Adams

Baker & Taylor

The First
Modern Olympics

A studio shot of Pierre Coubertin taken about 1894, when he first proposed modern Olympic Games.

The First

Modern Olympics

by

Richard D. Mandell

University of California Press
Berkeley • Los Angeles • London

University of California Press
Berkeley and Los Angeles, California

University of California Press, Ltd.
London, England

Copyright © 1976 by
The Regents of the University of California

ISBN: 0-520-02983-6
Library of Congress Catalog Card Number: 75-3773
Printed in the United States of America

an Professor Hajo Bernett

CONTENTS

PREFACE

This book describes and discusses the origins of the modern Olympic Games. The first chapter is about sport in ancient Greek society. The next deals with the *idea* of the Olympic Games which survived after the Games themselves were discontinued. The third chapter presents a portrait of the real hero of the book, Baron Pierre de Coubertin, the first impresario of international amateur sport. Much of what follows concerns the preparations for, and the actual unfolding of, the Games in Athens in 1896. The final chapter discusses the importance of that first modern Olympics for subsequent international athletic festivals.

Parts of this story have been told before. I share the enthusiasm of earlier writers on the subject, but I wish to tell more than a sports story. The modern Olympics are rooted in the culture of the nineteenth century and are a product of that century's intellectual dynamism and courage. Thus the spirit of the time, the social background and nineteenth-century organizational techniques, must all be evoked and described at least in part. Naturally I shall focus much attention on the young people— Greek, American, English, Hungarian, French, German, and others—who were the athletic heroes at the Athens Games, but I shall discuss ideologues, bureaucrats, and politicians who promoted international sport and to whom fans of the modern Olympics owe a large debt.

To understand how the Olympic Games came about as a

means of determining and rewarding the world's best athletes, we must familiarize ourselves with a milieu quite different from today's sweat-smelling gymnasiums or sunlit playing fields with their attendant joggers and coaches. In the period 1870–1914, the civilized world was going through demographic, technological, political, social, and intellectual transformations. European culture was simultaneously approaching its zenith and its apocalypse. (Though they all form part of the background, many major trends of late nineteen-century life must remain outside this story. We will not deal with intellectual wreckers or master builders, nor with such *fin de siècle* excesses as great wealth, indulged sensuality, or irresponsible political ambition. Nor will we be concerned with the multiplying, voting, ever more literate and self-conscious masses of Europe and America.)

Most of the characters in our story (apart from the athletes) were congenial, well-meaning, second-rank intellectuals, academicians, and bureaucrats. They were active members of the upper bourgeoisie. They lived well. They paid no income taxes and had only heard mention (whereupon they shuddered) of inflation. Their servants waxed the wainscoting, soaped the leather easy chairs, and dusted the gimcracks in their large, overfilled houses. The gentlemen exchanged long, penned letters that were rich in classical allusions, since the writers had learned as youths from Greek and Latin literary models. The tables of their libraries held fat reviews like *Century Magazine*, *Blackwood's*, *Le Revue des Deux Mondes*, or *Correspondance*. They traveled first-class on Europe's trains, cradled in mohair and shielded by frosted glass. Responsive stewards tended them as they lolled, reading, on chaises by the rails of ocean liners. Their common street costume was a black worsted, tailed, shaped suit which was specially brushed, pressed, and boutonnièred for the era's rites of passage, the banquets.

Long before the banquets were due to take place the competitive chefs of the great hotels drew up the menus. The menus were engraved and sometimes even tasseled. A respectable menu would list cultural as well as gastronomic events. The guests at these banquets would advance through soups, seafoods, meats, fowl, vegetables in thick sauces, desserts of layered, filled, and ornamented pastries, fruits, and cigars. The wines began light and faintly aromatic, became maroon and astringent and then heavily perfumed and syrupy before the diners dawdled over stinging brandy. The witty interjections of toastmasters forced laggards to keep up. Music and hired singers eased digestion. Speeches from the head table dealt with the special interests of the *convives* (the French word must be used here). A banquet might consist of six hours of calories, entertainment, and serious debate or oratory.

The banquet was just one technique used by Coubertin to accomplish his objectives. Though born into the old aristocracy, he was, by choice, a Republican. After 1880 or so, Republicanism was the only political ideology that would permit one to move effectively on several levels of French public life. Coubertin professed to favor social mobility and sneered at the ossified nobility everywhere. Significantly, however, he cherished titled "names" to serve as "honorary members" of his committees because their lingering cachet reassured (and sometimes even intimidated) so many of the bourgeoisie. And, in his own name, he kept the title "Baron" and the preposition "de" to the end.

The baron was flexible. He used many means of persuasion: letters to the editor, subsidized articles in magazines, pretentious assemblies in great halls redolent of history. Coubertin was also an opportunist. He convened "congresses" of "societies" which he had assembled, mostly out of nothing, and named only shortly before. Coubertin might cite bogus statistics or, for those he wished to impress, arrange a reception to be attended by a head of state or a cabinet minister. He could arrange a torchlit parade, a procession of yachts down the Seine, a lunch in a formal garden or, of course a banquet punctuated by speeches to stir the *convives* to acclamation when presented with Coubertin's schemes. In short, Coubertin was an inspired administrator.

He was also a French patriot. To Coubertin, the crucial event in modern history was France's defeat by Germany in 1870. His self-assigned crusade was to regenerate France by means of modern education. The new educational programs would revitalize French youths by strengthening their bodies as well as training their minds. He regularly devised school programs or model curricula for France and, later, for the world. His projects for international sport were originally intended to benefit France by exposing French youths and educators to the competition of young men from more advanced sporting nations.

The detailed scenes in the book take place far away from the grand stage of European history. Indeed, the first modern Olympic Games were puny compared with the more recent extravaganzas. The first festival in Athens occurred on the periphery of Europe. The athletic victors were, with some exceptions, themselves from the fringes of the Western world. Still, for a number of reasons that merit examination, the 1896 Games were well staged and had significant results—much more so than the next several Olympic festivals.

The period dealt with here is Europe before the Great War. Several characteristics of this work follow from its chronological cut-off point. For pictures I have relied almost entirely on the work of two especially deft magazine illustrators of the time. Corvin Knapp Linson (1864-1959) and Andrè Castaigne (active in Paris 1889-1930) were better able to suggest physical prowess and beauty than photographers could. Scrapbook photos of the heroes of 1896 are retrievable, but these studio shots with wicker chairs and potted palms make the young heroes look like effigies. And, as this book is about organizers as well as performers, I have included a photograph of Coubertin.

My high regard for the sportsmen has led me to include in the final chapter the statistics of performance at the 1896 Olympics, although to set forth the verdicts of stopwatches and tape measures at that time might shrink the stature of the book's heroes. Training and coaching were then in their infancy, particularly in Greece. Besides, eighty years ago, record-setting had not become the obsession it is now.

I should also say a word about the relative value of the currency of the period. In the early 1890s the French franc and the Greek drachma were about equal in value, though the drachma had depreciated 40 percent shortly before the 1896 Games. At the time, the franc exchanged for about five to the dollar, but the reader can assume that the purchasing power of both the franc and the drachma were a little greater than our present dollar.

It should be mentioned, too, that during this period Greece and the other countries of the Eastern Orthodox Church used the Julian calendar whose dates were twelve days behind those of the Gregorian calendar of the Catholics in the West. According to the Greek calendar, the Games in Athens were scheduled to begin on March 24, 1896, whereas by the calendar of western Europe they were to start on April 5. I have used the dates of the modern calendar throughout.

Some acknowledgments: This work was supported in part by the University of South California Research and Productive Scholarship Fund. I completed the book in the course of a Fulbright Fellowship in Germany during the year 1973-1974. The staffs at the Sportwissenschaftliches Institute of the University of Bonn and the Historisches Seminar of the Sporthochschule in Cologne were especially helpful. Once again it is a pleasure to thank the reference librarians at my university, the New York Public Library, the Library of Congress, and elsewhere. Some of my colleagues read and commented on earlier versions of my manuscript. They are: Jerry Augostinos, Bradley

Bargar, Peter Becker, Jim Cochrane, Susan Cochrane, Michael Lagrone, Temple Ligon, "Hamp" Smith, and Mike Smith. This is my first book that has been assisted in its progress by the editorial skills of my older daughters, Victoria and Eleanor. My gratitude to Elizabeth Ellen Kehr is transcendent.

1

THE OLYMPIC GAMES IN ANTIQUITY

*T*HE CLASSICAL GREEKS usually assumed that Hercules founded their most prestigious religious and sporting festival. Other traditions held that athletic competitions at Olympia in the eastern Peloponnesus were first held as part of the observances at the funeral of a local hero, Pelops.[1] In any case, archaeological investigations at Olympia in the nineteenth century exposed altars and votive offerings from Mycenean times.[2] Though the first recorded Olympic victory was that of Coroebus, a sprinter from Elis, in 776 B.C., athletic contests at Olympia were probably adjuncts of much older festivals in honor of Zeus. By the time Greek hegemony in the eastern Mediterranean in the fifth century, the sacred grove at Olympia was the most holy site of Panhellenic significance.

The content of the athletic festival varied over its thousand-year history, but not much. The prestige of the Olympic Games was so great and their integration into Greek religious life was so taken for granted as to discourage tampering with their order and ritual. It may be useful here to describe a typical festival at Olympia during a time of political calm in the fifth century B.C.[3] The monuments at Olympia and the festival itself were under the official care of Elis, a small city-state or polis, which the more powerful Greek states purposefully kept neutral and insignificant. Every fourth year in the spring, three heralds set out from Elis to cover routes through the whole Greek world. As the heralds arrived at each city-state or colony, they proclaimed a sacred truce. Thereafter competitors or spectators traveling to or from Olympia were under the official protection of Zeus. Considering the Greeks' combativeness, this truce was observed with remarkably few exceptions.

Upon arriving safely at Olympia, the athletes and their trainers were at once put under the supervision of Elian judges who decided on their eligibility. The competitors had to prove that they were of pure Greek blood. The judges might decide that the declared age of a youth was too low and would therefore rule that he could not enter in the boys' events, but would instead have to compete as a man. Since the holy site attracted relatively few pilgrims, except during the grand festival, the sports fields were overgrown with weeds and had to be cleared. The infield of the stadium had to be covered with a smooth layer of fresh sand. The athletes themselves did this work.

Eventually a growing stream of visitors crowded Olympia and its surroundings. Delegations from proud cities vied in the loudness of their cheering sections and in the openness with which they displayed their gifts of art works to Zeus or to Hera, Zeus's wife, who was also especially honored at Olympia. Cities whose athletes had been victorious in the previous festival ceremoniously added commemorative statues to those already crowding the altis, a sacred enclosure containing temple and altars. On hand were hawkers of small, votive statues for people who might wish to demonstrate more modestly their devotion at Olympia's sanctuaries. Colonists from the Black Sea, Africa, and Sicily used the gathering to exchange reminiscences or to sign business deals with tourists from their mother cities in Attica or Lydia. Kings, tyrants, and chief magistrates from various parts of the Greek world used the guarantee of safety and the euphoric ambiance at Olympia to conclude treaties. There were also performing jugglers, magicians, and sooth-sayers. Peddlers sold snacks or souvenirs. Poets cultivating Panhellenic reputations would establish themselves in the colonnades of temples and there read aloud their newest works. A philosopher, Thales of Miletus, was one of the rare casualties at Olympia. Aged 78, he died there owing to heat and thirst during the 58th Olympics in 548 B.C.

The hosts from tiny Elis were in no position to provide adequate housing for the many thousands who came. The only plumbing consisted of a few springs and the nearby rivers. Wealthy visitors or delegations desiring to leave an enduring impression brought pack trains laden with coffers of delicacies, as well as tents which they had decorated with embroidered tapestries. However, at night most visitors, athletes included, simply wrapped themselves up in their cloaks, lay down, and went to sleep looking at the moon and the constellations. The number of visitors at the festival was usually much larger than could fit into the stadium for track and field events. The stadium held roughly 40,000 people, standing and sitting; there were no seats.

For centuries the holy site at the base of the Kronion hill and the junction of the Kladeos and Alpheios rivers was little more than a pretty field with a few sacrificial altars and the roughly marked boundaries of a stadium and a hippodrome. Characteristically, the Spartans were the first to monumentalize their athletic prominence. Late in the seventh century B.C. they built a large, Doric temple of stone to Hera. By the fifth century B.C. the gifts of statuary, treasure houses, and temples had so crowded the altis that it had to be enlarged. The site of the stadium was twice shifted to the east.

The grandest monument at Olympia was the fifth-century temple to Zeus. Its stuccoed, shell limestone exterior sheltered Phidias's colossal statue of the father of the gods. Somewhat larger than a two-story house, the statue of the enthroned god was composed of a framework supporting a light exterior of carved and polished ivory, gold, ebony, and precious stones. When first seen from the great doors of the temple, the statue seemed to glow with a light of its own. Phidias' Zeus dazzled all visitors and was probably the most admired work of art in classical antiquity.

During the centuries of Olympia's great importance as a Panhellenic festival, the celebrations at Olympia occupied five days of the second or third (alternately) full moon after the summer solstice—that is, from the twelfth to the sixteenth of August or September.[4] The first day was given over to oaths, sacrifices, the singing of hymns, and other religious observances. There was no attempt at any time to gather all those present at Olympia for a general ceremony. Some athletes offered gifts or prayers before victory statues of athletes who had been deified or at shrines of various patron gods, including several statues of Zeus. According to the account of Pausanius,

the Zeus of the Council Chamber is of all the images of Zeus the one most likely to strike terror into the hearts of sinners. He is surnamed the Oath-God, and in each hand he holds a thunderbolt. Beside this image it is customary for athletes, their fathers and their brothers as well as their trainers, to swear an oath upon slices of boars' flesh that in nothing will they sin against the Olympic Games.[5]

The sports competitions began on the second day. In the morning most of those present gathered at the hippodrome, a cleared, leveled, narrow oval about 500 meters long, east of the altis, south of the stadium, and north of the bed (at that time) of the river Alpheios. The most prestigious event was the race for quadrigae, light, two-wheeled chariots pulled by four horses. Since the number of entries was large, sometimes reaching more than forty teams, there were elaborate, staggered starting gates leading into the oval. The course was not around a track with curved ends, but around two columns separated by about four hundred meters. The distance was twelve laps—that is, twenty-four times the distance between the two columns. However, since the drivers had to swing wide, the distance traveled was somewhat longer than the distance of nearly 10,000 meters or six miles that simple multiplication gives us. Tactics and control were critical at the turns. Immobilizing accidents were common—indeeed, usual. Once in a race for forty chariots there was but one finisher. At the end of the race the owner of the winning team of horses bound a fillet holding olive leaves about the head of the driver. Then the owner himself, as the Olympic victor, advanced to a gold and ivory table upon which were crowns of olive leaves that had been cut by a noble youth of Elis with a golden sickle from a sacred tree near the temple of Zeus. A herald shouted the owner's name, that of his father, and that of his polis, while a judge placed the victor's crown on his head. In ancient times the sport horse had about it a magical aura as a symbol of power which it has not quite lost to this day. So symbolically indicative of great wealth were race horses that merely to enter a chariot in a major festival was to establish oneself as a personage of note in the ancient world.

Next came the race for single horses with mounts. The jockeys competed naked (the chariot drivers wore a short tunic) and bareback, for saddles, stirrups, harnesses, and metal shoes were still unknown. The horses and riders, however, did not stir spectators, chroniclers, or artists as did the teams of four. Consequently, we have few literary records of the horse races. We are not even sure what distance the races covered. It could have been as little as four hundred meters—that is, one lap—or it could have been as much as six laps.

Even before the end of the victory ceremonies for the jockeys, many in the crowd were leaving for the grassy slopes of the stadium to observe the finalists in the pentathlon. In classical times the five events were the discus throw, the long jump, the javelin throw, the sprint, and wrestling. In formal Greek meets the field events were performed only as elements of the pentathlon. Some ancient sources suggest that decisive performances in the three field events were sufficient to determine a winner and that the sprint and the wrestling were performed only when the scores of the finalists were close.[6] The grace at full power of the athletes in the field events usually roused the massed spectators to raptures of admiration. The large, elegant pentathlon athlete was the one most likely to be watched and sketched by the sculptors.

During the evening of this second day of the great festival

there were sacrifices of black cattle at an ancient altar dedicated
to the mythical hero, Pelops. Flower-bedecked men chanted
hymns as they paraded by the light of the full moon around the
altis, before leaving for privately offered feasts and, much later,
their beds in the open air.

Most of the third day was taken up by ritual observances in
honor of the patron god. A long procession wound about the
sacred precinct and approached one of the holiest sites at
Olympia, a high mound of ashes called the Altar of Zeus.
Participators were Elian supervisors, priests, athletes and their
hangers-on, and servants leading cattle. Officials from distant
poleis carried gifts of finely worked, precious metals. On a
platform before this conical altar, closely watched priests
slaughtered one hundred beasts from which they at once
removed the thighs, which were then burned to ashes at the top
of the altar, the new ashes thus adding to the size of the altar.

The only athletic events of the third day were the three
footraces. The "distance event" in the ancient Olympics was
called the dolichos and consisted of twenty-four lengths of the
stadium field—there as in the hippodrome there was no oval or
round track—which was roughly two hundred meters long. As
many as twenty entrants, lined up at one end of the stadium and
at the start ran out to go around posts much as the horses did.
The proving of the superior runner depended very much on his
skill, amid equally determined opponents, in surviving abrupt
turns on a surface of loose sand. The long race offered the
spectacle of falls, shoving, and maneuvering for position; it was
not merely a demonstration of staying power and rhythmic
perfection. As with so many Greek athletic events, one suspects
that the race either developed or was devised in order to
produce a theatrical spectacle.

The dash of one stadium length, or stade, came next. The
victor in this event won, in addition to his olive wreath, a
particular kind of immortality. Among Greek historians after
the middle of the fourth century B.C. the Panhellenic chrono-

logical system, which gradually replaced the several previously existing Greek chronologies, consisted of a series of four-year periods called Olympiads (the great festival itself was not an Olympiad). Each Olympiad took the name of the victorious sprinter at the Olympic Games which had inaugurated the period.

The last footrace on the third day, called the diaulos, was an event of two stadium lengths. The line of runners dug their toes into grooves chiseled in a row of marble slabs that were set into the ground and which made up the starting line. At the blast of a trumpet they made for the column two hundred meters away, rounded it, and rushed back to the start. As was customary at the stadium, the spectators were noisily enthusiastic.

Then the athletes, their entourages, and the spectators went off to a large feast which, though it certainly was pervaded by a mood of high revelry, had cultish overtones. It was assumed that at this banquet Zeus himself was present in unseen form. The food was primarily the roasted carcasses of the sacrificial cattle slaughtered that morning.

The fourth day was given over to what the Greeks called the "heavy" events. Three were combative sports. Two of these could be compared with our modern wrestling and boxing, and the third was called the the pancration. Though we know rather well how one trained for and competed in these sports, we do not know how many finalists actually competed in the Olympics, nor whether the bouts were held at the stadium or somewhere within the altis. It seems likely that the spectators at Olympia would probably have preferred to see only the most notorious fighters, particularly in the pancration, which allowed more holds, blows, and kicks, and which required more refined training than either wrestling or boxing. The Elians may have supervised elimination rounds before the festival proper began and the finals themselves may have been observed only by small groups of special judges. But here the archaeological or literary sources for final judgments are lacking.[7]

A fourth "heavy" event was the race of two stadium lengths for foot soldiers. The tough hoplites, or heavily armored foot soldiers, were the basic units of the Greek phalanx and were the foundation, therefore, of the Greek armies. The competitors were naked like the other athletes except that they wore helmets and shin guards and carried shields.

The fifth and last day of the festival at Olympia was given over to more processions, ritual celebrations, and banquets. The Olympic victors, in addition to their olive crowns, wore circlets of flowers and trailed ribbons as they thanked Zeus for their triumphs. Lines of boys, men, and elders danced to the melodies and rhythms of harps, flutes, and drums. There was another feast at which more sacrificed animals were eaten. Then the people prepared for their journeys back to the disparate parts of the Greek world, a world that had been peacefully and joyously—but, alas, only briefly—united at holy Olympia.

The most precious cargo the city delegations could take home was one or more Olympic victors. At Olympia itself the victor received only symbolic indications that he had been favored by Zeus. Once home he led yet more processions. He was a subject for odes by local lyricists. He got commodity payments, cash, and pensions. His deeds were inscribed in the temples. He was memorialized by conventionally idealized statues of athletes. An especially marvelous athlete—one who spread the reputation of his city by winning in successive Olympics or in other major athletic festivals—might be memorialized by a statue made in his own image.

An athletic victory was accepted as evidence of something much grander than the confirmation of a pure physical skill. To a people ruled by competing, capricious gods, it was an unequivocal indication of heavenly favor for the athlete, his family, and his polis as well. The Greeks had proof of the gods' interference in athletic contests in the *Iliad* and the *Odyssey*.[8] A victory at Olympia, and only slightly less so at the Pythian Games at Delphi or the Isthmian or Nemean Games (to name the four major athletic festivals of the later Greek world), was confirmation that rituals had been correctly performed, that prayers had been heard and heeded. The victorious athlete was, therefore, a harbinger of good fortune. Significantly, the classical Greeks abandoned the practice, apparent in Homer's epics, of awarding second, third, and subsequent prizes. Many poleis, and especially those in south Italy and Sicily, made strenuous efforts to obtain athletic victors. They recruited athletes and trainers, investigated the scientific principles of high performance, built luxurious training facilities, bribed judges, sacrificed lavishly, and prayed. There was an uninterrupted tendency from the sixth century onward for training to become more intense and for aristocratic amateurs to abandon participation in the major meets to single-minded, paid specialists— in short, professionals.

As the generations passed there was also a tendency for religious festivals with athletic meets incorporated in them to proliferate wherever Greek culture had penetrated. The various festivals were dedicated to many gods. The victors' crowns were of laurel, pine, wild celery, or other herbs. Some festivals, in addition to the conventional athletic events, had accompanying competitions in poetry, music, or other arts. The hosts, sacerdotal and civil, assumed that a festival brought prestige to local temples and pleased the Panhellenic and local gods. A class of itinerant, professional athletes and trainers became increasingly sought after (as well as painfully arrogant). The stadiums, gymnasiums, and palaestras (wrestling schools) of Greece became ever more numerous, larger, and more the focal points of public life. The presentation of individual athletic events, as well as the festivals themselves, became more theatrical and lavish. For centuries the Greeks were the most sports-minded people the world has ever known.

A peculiar characteristic of antique Greek sport was that athletes trained and competed naked, a practice that the Spartans were supposed to have originated. The sportsmen in

Homer's time wore shorts. The nakedness of the Greeks, incidentally, was a hindrance to the acceptance of their sport by the more prudish Hebrews and Romans. But then perhaps one should qualify "naked." A reader of the literary sources for Greek sport is struck by the role that olive oil and powders played in the lives of athletes. Before training or competing the athletes usually smeared themselves or each other with oil and then sprinkled their bodies with mineral or vegetable powders that were believed to help heat dispersion and strength retention, and to have other prized qualities.[9] For the wrestlers and pancratists, certain powders aided their holds and registered with certainty the occurrence of a fall.

Greek sport was less complex and various than modern sport, but it was probably more integrated into daily life. I have emphasized the role of athletics in religious and civic ceremonies and in the Greek desire for fame. I have also mentioned the theatrical presentation of sport at the festivals. I should add here that many agonistic events such as the weapons race and the pancration were done to musical accompaniment. Were they, then, forms of dance? We do know that various kinds of dance were also agonistically practiced before judges at certain cult celebrations in the Greek world.

As with so many aspects of high Greek culture, watching and participating in festively staged sport were almost exclusively privileges of males.[10] The gymnasium, a large colonnaded complex for training in many sports, and the palaestra, a smaller building provided so Greeks could practice their favorite participatory sport, wrestling, were also meeting places where youths and older men gathered for workouts, conversation, and homoerotic looking and assignations.[11] Some gymnasiums were preferred as the sketching studios for artists. The aestheticized, praised, and much-practiced homoeroticism, which was integrated into Greek education and morals, was surely a basis for the stylistic advances of the Greek sculptors who had originally been inspired by their Egyptian, Mesopotamian, and Cretan predecessors.

We have long known that the events of Greek sport were in many ways different from comparable events in the modern sports program.[12] Relative to the track and field program, I have already noted that the athletes ran naked over loose sand and for distances that were multiples of the stade, a stadium length. The length of a stadium varied, but was usually about two hundred meters. For races of two stades or more the competitors made 180-degree turns around posts. Military, diplomatic, and business affairs all demanded that the Greeks cultivate long-distance joggers for urgent intercity communications, but we have no record of a sporting race longer than three miles. Perhaps the wretched appearance of the long distance runner at the end of this race offended the Greeks' often-disobeyed maxim, "Nothing in excess," as well as their canons of male physical beauty. The spare, sinewy men who are successful distance runners were never models for the sculptors who preferred the Heracles-like sprinters, wrestlers, and experts in the field events.

There were, of course, no speed records nor do we have many statistical records of exceptional performances of strength or dexterity. Victors were always determined in proximate combat. On the other hand, much talent and energy were devoted to the improvement of athletic performance. Experiments demonstrated that hand-held stones or castings, correctly carried and swung, could lengthen the distance of the standing long jump. These halteres, which varied in weight and form, were fixtures at track and field meets. Similarly, the trainers improved the expected maximum performances with the tossed spear by providing the athlete with a leather thong wrapped about the shaft which gave it increased thrust and spin after it left the thrower's hand. Discuses were made of stone or were metal castings, and they were of various weights, though they would be standardized at an important meet. The discus thrower's technique was much like the rising spin familiar to modern athletes and fans.

The three Greek combative sports—boxing, wrestling, and

pancration—must be briefly noted. Boxers wore no mitts, but they did wrap their fists in soft leather thongs in order to protect them. Wrestlers were severely limited in the holds they could use. A pancratist, on the other hand, could kick and do just about anything else except gouge. At the Nemean Games of about 400 B.C. Damoxenus of Syracuse astonished Creugas of Epidamnus with an open-handed jab into the stomach which ripped his entrails out. It was a dreadful foul, and Creugas, who died on the spot, was awarded the victor's crown posthumously. There were no rounds. The fights just went on until the weaker man gave up. This fact, plus the increasing professionalization of Greek Sport, often made the prestigious contests dreadfully long and boring. The professional wrestler or pancratist who wished to survive in order to perform again assiduously avoided any contact that could be maiming. He would dance about until his opponent dropped his guard, and then he would rush in to end the fight quickly. A fight lasting a day or more might end when the weaker and still untouched fighter raised his finger to the judge, signifying defeat and a desire to sleep.

Many, perhaps almost all, of the ancient peoples played some sort of ball games. Egyptian wall paintings show what can only be hockey sticks, carried by what look like teams of players playing with various kinds of balls which were presumably hustled by cooperative effort from one goal to another. We have various literary allusions to Greeks juggling or throwing balls competitively. Team sports, however, with their time periods, rules, and cooperative specialized players, had no place in the Greek festivals, which demanded supreme efforts by individuals alone.[13] Nor did the Greeks have relay races in their meets. As for swimming, we know that the Greeks swam and dived in their rivers and along their coasts, and that swimming was one of the skills that a responsible Greek father was expected to teach his children. Most pictorial representations of water sports show Greeks doing the sidestroke or in the midst of swan dives. While there must have been informal swimming races, we have no records to suggest that there were standard courses, that performances were staged before spectators, or that very good swimmers could acquire lasting prestige.[14]

Even if we include the equestrian events, it should be apparent that the formal, classical athletic program (that is, leaving out ball play, swimming, and other recreational activities which have left only scarce pictorial or literary records) was rather limited. It should also be pointed out that the satisfaction derived from Greek athletic training, competition, and observation were for long confined to the leisured aristocracy. The admission of lowborn professionals to athletic events at the great festivals, and their eventual domination of those events, were a consequence of the extremely high value the Greeks placed upon an athletic victory which took place in the setting of a cult festival. Aristocrats just would not take the trouble. The athletes who performed in events that were adjuncts of the religious celebrations had, besides training devotedly, pleaded intensely for celestial assistance. Many athletes probably competed in a religious trance. In fact, the ritualistic setting of the formal athletic meet helps to explain the astonishing longevity of the Olympic program. The occasional appearance of events for boys and races for mule pairs, or the clumsy tampering with the Olympic program by some Romans, should not obscure the fact that for a thousand years at Olympia (and for shorter periods at other regular festivals) the program changed very little.

Until modern times the Greeks were unique in that exceptional prowess in sport could furnish the raw material for heroes accepted by the society at large. Athletic distinction was a common subject for great Hellenic poetry and art. Artistic representations of supreme male beauty appeared in Greek vase paintings, carved jewels, metal work, and statuary. And though it rarely or only briefly worked out in practice, sport—or at least regular, planned physical training—was an integral part of many educational schemes advanced by Greek philosophers to improve or reform their society.[15] There were critics of sport, especially in Hellenistic times, but they objected mainly to the arrogant, overindulged professional athletes and their hangers-on, not to physical education itself or to the sporting festivals.[16]

Sport was not only integrated in the lives and spirit of the most dazzlingly original and impressive civilization the world has ever known, but it has been accepted by all philhellenes (in more or less biased form) that this was so. Much more debatable is whether this unique integration of sport and culture explains, even partially, the stunning intellectual innovations of the Greeks. This question is one that has preoccupied many scholars, social critics, and educators, particularly since the eighteenth century.

What is not questionable is that Greek sport left its mark on other Mediterranean civilizations. Though commercial and political rivals of the Hellenes, the Etruscans adopted into their art the Greeks' depictions of sport. (Remember that Greek artworks were also items of merchandise that energetic Greek traders took with them on their expeditions.) Etruscan artists sometimes even reproduced track and field events in their own art without understanding them.[17] Clumsy depictions of Greek boxers, runners, and spectators appeared on the hammered metal work of tribes in what is modern Yugoslavia.[18] Even long after Greek political hegemony had passed, it was assumed necessary for a city to possess stadiums, hippodromes, gymnasiums, and palaestras to prove that it was a part of the civilized world. (Typically, and in opposition to the orthodox practice in Jerusalem, the Hellenizing high priest, Jason, established in 174 B.C. a gymnasium where the participants were naturally expected to practice nude. Some of the more cosmopolitan Jewish athletes, according to the first book of Maccabees [1:15], actually underwent cosmetic operations to conceal the fact that they were circumcised.)

When the Romans took over the task of uniting Italy from the Etruscans, they were essentially without high culture, but their steady accretion of power, along with their wealth and their growing leisured class, left them open to seduction by the sophisticated Greeks whom they had conquered. Sport, rather broadly considered, had for centuries been an inseparable part of the great package that made up Greek culture: the Romans took some parts of this package and rejected others. A most important invention of the Romans was a military one, the legion. To prepare for service in the legions of the Republic, the conscripted citizen-soldiers had to practice synchronized marching and fighting with the sword. But their practice was purposeful preparation and not an end in itself. Roman fathers were admonished to teach their sons to swim, to run, and in general to be physically tough, but this was character building, not sport. Nevertheless they did take over and adapt certain aspects of Greek sport, owing in part, no doubt, to their passion for spectacle.

Curiously, it is mostly from Roman polemics that we know that many Romans were either disturbed or seduced by Greek sport. For example, Romans were not supposed to go about naked, and the fact that the Greeks assiduously cultivated suntans, which they displayed in toto at every opportunity, permitted some Romans to class them with the dusky Syrians and Egyptians for whom they had no respect. The first Greek athletes in Rome were professionals brought over by a promoter of spectacles in 186 B.C. When they stripped for their performances they shocked the spectators. That nudity which the Hellenes considered healthy and flattering was later called by Cicero "the beginning of evildoing." Still, the frequent alarm expressed by Roman social critics about expenditures for oil and prices for athletes, and the critics' sneers at the idlers who gathered at the gymnasiums would tend to indicate that large numbers of Romans found pleasure in these very activities. Likewise, when Cicero says it is "disgraceful" for Roman citizens to go off to the games at Olympia when there are crises at home, we know that some, at least, of those citizens must have gone.[19]

Many cultivated Romans were well aware of the value of the best works of Greek art and yearned to possess them. Neither plunder nor purchase satisfied the keen demand for sculpture. Eventually Roman entrepreneurs sketched or made casts of famous originals and hired Greek craftsmen to reproduce them, so that most of what we can now see of classical Greek sculpture are only products of Roman factories. Myron's "Discobolus," for one, exists only through copies. Our few originals of Greek athletic sculpture are pathetic remnants of the swarms of statues that once enriched the sites of the sports festivals. While the "Charioteer of Delphi," the boy jockey from Artemisium, and the large bronze "Zeus Hurling a Thunderbolt" (sometimes called "Poseidon Hurling a Trident")—all recently recovered and all now viewable in Athens—compel our admiration, none of these works was considered worthy of the artist's signature at the time it was produced and none was distinguished enough to rate a description by either Greek or Roman chroniclers.

In the early days of the empire the Romans became more keenly interested in Olympia. Part of the imperial policy of Augustus (27 B.C.–A.D. 14) was to restore the old festivals in Greece. New athletic festivals were also established in Naples, Pergamum, Alexandria, and Laodicea. To celebrate his victory over Antony and Cleopatra at Actium in 31 B.C., Augustus instituted an "Actian" festival intended to rival the one in Olympia. And since the long-standing custom among historians in the Greek world had been to reckon time in four-year Olympiads, for a while Augustus even tried to institute a new pan-Mediterranean calendar of five-year "Actiads."[20]

Olympia also figured in the lives of later emperors. Tiberius (A.D. 14–37) avoided public appearances as an old man, but as a youth he had been an Olympic victor in the four-horse chariot race at Olympia. The most hysterical enthusiast for Greek athletics was Nero (A.D. 54–68). It suited Nero's convenience during a visit to Greece that there be irregular "Olympic Games" in A.D. 67, a non-Olympic year, in which he himself

competed in specially established competitions for actors and
for cithera players. He also drove in the two– and four–horse
chariot races. In a unique event, the conceiving of which
confounds the visual imagination today, he drove a ten-horse
team, presumably one of several in the race, before his chariot.
To the astonishment of nobody, the young emperor—as actor,
musician, and athlete—was uniformly triumphant. A later
generation of Elian officials ordered Nero's name stricken from
the victors' lists and annulled the Games ordered by their
bribed predecessors.

Tiberius Claudius Herodes Atticus (ca. A.D. 101–177), a
Roman born near Athens and possibly the wealthiest man in
antiquity, was the most conspicuous benefactor of Greece. He
had served the emperor Hadrian as an administrator in Asia but
is mostly remembered for how he got rid of his enormous riches.
He restored old buildings or gave new ones to Delphi, Ther-
mopolae, Corinth, and many other cities in the eastern Mediterranean. He considered building a canal through the isthmus
at Corinth, but was discouraged by Nero's earlier, unsuccessful
attempt. As one might expect of an enthusiastic philhellene,
Herodes Atticus was also especially generous to Olympia, the
Panhellenic center for sport, and to Athens, whose universal
significance for philosophy and art he recognized.

That the stadium and the hippodrome at Olympia retained
their rustic form during the prosperous days of the Pax Romana
is testimony to the steadfast conservatism of the priests and
aristocrats of nearby Elis who remained in control.[21] Herodes
Atticus had been a spectator at the Olympic Games and had
read his poetry and debated philosophical issues in the altis
there. We can almost envisage a scene in which he pleaded in
vain with a committee of Elian elders for the opportunity to
spruce up the weedy stadium in order to approach Roman
standards of splendor. The Elians did permit Herodes Atticus to
end at last the notorious shortage of drinking water at Olympia.
He had a three-kilometer-long aqueduct built from a stream

leading to the Alpheios. Where the aqueduct disgorged at the north wall of the altis, the millionaire donated a showy, marble housing for the fountain. This "Nyphaeum" consisted of basins, colonnades, allegorical reliefs, and festoons. Other ornaments consisted of statues of the imperial family and of Herodes Atticus and his wife. His donations to Athens were grander. His gift of the Odeon, a Roman-style theater, partially hollowed out of the rock at the base of the Acropolis, was a monument to his wife. Another gift was a magnificent stadium.

Although Athens was not noted for producing great athletes, she had long had her own athletic festival, the Panathenaea, which for centuries rivaled in prestige many other important festivals of sub-Olympic rank. In Athens the prizes for victory were large, painted vases, the Panathenaic amphorae, many of which have survived. When presented as awards, the vases were filled with the best olive oil from Attica. These athletic festivals in Athens were accompanied with much informal heartiness and, occasionally, disorder. Xenophon notes in his *Hipparchios* that horsemen had to be ranged in front of crowds at reviews and races in order to prevent the excited mobs from invading the course.

Though the prizes for victory at the games in Athens were valuable, for centuries the standard of presentation remained rather simple. A considerable proportion of Athenian public wealth, in keeping with the city's reputation, was spent on more temples and theaters, while other and poorer cities built solid stadiums. Athens had a permanent stadium only after about 330 B.C., when the orator Lycurgus, who had built the first stone theater in Athens, took charge of the city's finances for twelve years. Although in decline as a world power, Athens was enjoying a long period of peace after her wars with Philip of Macedon. The new stadium was to be built on land donated by a certain Deinias for the purpose. The site was a deep ravine at a right angle to the river Ilissus. The natural declivity was formed by the Ardettus hill and a hill opposite that were joined by a high saddle about three hundred meters from the river. The site, then, was a large natural amphitheater with greatly lengthened sides. Excavations, fillings, and shapings produced a level, narrow infield and a track with the customary sharp turns at the ends. The sloped sides accommodated more than 50,000 spectators. A little later the field received inset stone blocks to mark starting and finishing lines and a drainage system for rainwater. There was also a parapet to separate the contestants from the spectators who lounged or squatted on the steep slopes (wooden benches being provided only for high dignitaries). As today, a seat on those hills offered a view not only of the activities below, but of the Acropolis (little more than a mile away), Lykabettus, Hymettus, Pentilicus, Parnes, and the bright temples elsewhere in the city. Over all was the friendly sun and the clear air. And thus were the Panathenaic games celebrated for some five hundred years.

About 143 B.C. Herodes Atticus was chosen as agonothete, or supervisor, of the Panathenaic games. As he was ceremoniously crowned as an official in the old stadium, he grandly announced to the crowd, "At your next gathering here, I promise you a stadium of marble." He kept his promise, and all later travelers enthusiastically praised the new stadium. The entire area used by the spectators had been covered with stepped ranges of Pentelic slabs upon which were benches, also of marble. Atop the great arc of the closed end of the arena (called the sphendone) was a small colonnaded temple and a sweeping, curved portico. The whole structure was about two hundred meters long and about forty meters wide and seated from 45,000 to 70,000 people (both the crush and the estimates varied). There were changing rooms and baths for the athletes. There were also pens and long tunnels for the introduction of gladiators and beasts, for the Romans had successfully introduced the circus and the gladiatorial spectacle to Greece. In these late days of Athens's glory, a time when grandeur and luxury were what most excited the travelers and chroniclers, the bas-reliefs, bronze moldings, and other decorations at the stadium were considered outstanding. Posts and various starting and finishing lines were marked by marble steles in traditional styles and of the finest workmanship. The many ornaments and statues were done in high classical style, a style already of great age and considered unimprovable. The new stadium in Athens surpassed Rome's Colosseum and the Circus Maximus in elegance if not in size, and, though not in competition with the Parthenon (which was six hundred years older), it was certainly one of Athens's more harmonious large structures. It was also the last important architectural addition to ancient Athens.

The stadium was kept in good repair for centuries. It witnessed the degeneration of sporting competitions into gruesome extravaganzas that pandered to the debased tastes of the later Romans. We have records of the front seats being inadvertently sprinkled with the blood of humans who were murdered in the course of the circuses that were festively integrated into late Roman culture. A late alteration at the stadium was an iron grating to protect the crowds from frightened and enraged African beasts. One Roman emperor presented the jaded Athenians with an especially grand spectacle that required the slaughter of a thousand wild animals.

Did the Romans participate in sport? Though some Romans practiced at the gymnasiums, and a few eccentrics competed in the Greek festivals, the Roman moralists frowned on participation in idle sport as being bad for the character. The occasional inclusion of professional athletes in Roman public entertainments was done either to revel in philhellene sentiment or to provide novelties. Of course, many elegant Romans adored the whole complex of classical Greek culture, which had been considerably glamorized over the centuries after Pericles, and to do so required that they profess enthusiasm for classical Greek athletics. Thus the interest of the emperors Hadrian (A.D. 117–138) and Marcus Aurelius (A.D. 161–180) in Olympia and in Greek sport must be assumed to be a part of their more pervasive nostalgia for classical Greece as a whole.

The Roman propensity for sadism and luxury, and a bored yearning for novelty, all of which the Greeks tried to keep out of their formal sports, were catered to by the Romans. Chariot racing and gladitorial contests, for example, were both Roman enthusiasms. Indeed, the Roman interest in chariot racing was even keener than that of the Greeks. In the later days of the Roman empire there were rival stables, some of which were huge commercial enterprises. The colors (usually green and blue) worn by the drivers became loaded with symbolic burdens of such complexity and weight that race results provoked riots. The continued rivalry of the blues and the greens later triggered upheavals that threatened the stability of the Byzantine empire.

Some Roman historians claimed that the Romans had picked up the taste for gladitorial contests (as well as for chariot racing) from the cruel Etruscans. [22] In the early Republic, funerals of great men and, somewhat later, victories in war were celebrated and solemnized with ever increasing numbers of battles between professional showmen. The most famous of the special schools to train these condemned prisoners, slaves, and psychopaths was in Capua. [23] Theatrically staged battles became features of the Roman regime wherever it was imposed. While especially brave losers were sometimes spared, and a few especially skilled gladiators lived to train others and thus survived to old age, the point of attending such spectacles was, of course, to witness a ceremonial murder.

The rareness of any expressions of disgust over these displays, which took the lives of tens of thousands of men, testifies to their enormous popularity. Some Roman moralists actually recommended attendance at the gladitorial shows as a means of accustoming effete youths to the sight of carnage. There was a strange, erotic fascination with the despised gladiators, who ranked in social status with male prostitutes. Great significance was placed on their appearance in dreams.

The blood of a slain gladiator held magic properties. The fighters were announced with fanfares and battled with swords or other weapons to the accompaniment of flutes, drums, and choruses. For their spectators at the arenas the more munificent hosts of the contests offered sprays of perfumes and awnings as shades against the sun.

The human material for the gladitorial schools was difficult to locate, required longer training, and was consequently expensive for an impresario to purchase. Outlays were enormous for procuring gladiators and for tracking down Christians and other dissenters to be sacrificed, as were also the expenses necessary to capture and then to maintain in fighting trim lions, elephants, and other beasts. All this must have contributed to the material as well as the moral bankruptcy of the Roman system. Yet the circuses were difficult to eradicate even when most upper-class Romans had become Christians. In about A.D. 400 Saint Augustine recorded with horror his friend's enchantment at an arena. Shortly afterward the gladitorial shows were at last declared illegal, but the fights with animals were not abolished until A.D. 681.

Long before the centuries of Roman hegemony, baths were known in the East. Warm baths were sometimes attached to the Greek gymnasiums in Hellenistic times, but the Greek athlete usually cleansed himself of post-workout oil, grime, and sweat with the cupped, curved blade of the strigil, sometimes ending the process with a cold plunge into an available stream. Greek pedagogues and trainers tended to view warm baths as effeminizing and bath attendants as rogues. On the other hand, Roman citizens, even in the Republic, had private and later public warm baths. Plumbing technology, the flexibility of brick and mortar architecture, and the taste for luxury later led to elaborate establishments with swimming pools and hot and cold chambers.

It was not until imperial days that the great baths became integrated public policy. The increasing complexity and expense of the baths in the provinces, but especially in the capital, show that the emperors felt compelled to compete with their predecessors in extravagance. The vast remains of the baths of Caracalla (ca. A.D. 212) and Diocletian (ca. A.D. 302) are stunning today, but they only hint at their size and splendor when they were veneered with marbles and contained gymnasiums, courts for ball games, libraries, halls for theatrical performances, and little nooks for mischief.

The Christians did not, as has been claimed, oppose cleanliness, fitness, and sport. It was probably the destruction of the aqueducts by the Huns and the turning of the bath halls into churches, rather than any disgust at licentiousness, which caused the baths to be closed. Similarly, the fact that the arenas were sometimes sites of dramatic martyrdoms was vital in the claimed antiathleticism of the early Christian fathers. The panegyrists of modern sport have tended to set too sharply the contrast between supposedly widespread antique sport and supposedly nonexistent Christian sport. Christianity, they say, is hostile to the body.[24] Though festively staged and standardized antique sport ceased to exist in Europe, we can probably attribute this ending of a phase in sports history to the collapse of Roman civilization and to the Christian disgust with the festivals rather than to Christian objections to games and physical recreation as such.[25]

What happened to the Olympic Games during Rome's last centuries? During the Pax Romana the patronage of sentimental emperors and millionaires led to Olympia's greatest prosperity. Tourists went to see Phidias's statue of Zeus much as we make art pilgrimages to Chartres. To Olympia the Romans gave gymnasiums, hotels, athletic dormitories, and baths, which the Elians placed outside the altis. The program at the regular festivals varied little, and the Olympic truce (which, we recall, covered only travelers to and from Olympia and not the whole Greek world) was maintained. The racial standards for admission to the events were progressively loosened. Romans and then Africans and Asians were allowed to compete as athletes. The last Olympic victor of whom we have record was an Armenian prince, Varaztad, who won the boxing competitions in A.D. 385.

Long before this date, however, Olympia had lost all real meaning as a holy place. The ancient religious ceremonies were cynically observed and the competitions had no connection with actual Greek concerns.[26] As Roman energies declined, only their nostalgia and the prestige of the site kept the festivals going. The name "Olympia" itself was loosely used. Augustus had left an endowment to Antioch (in present-day Syria) for the establishment of a regular athletic festival. The games, which were presented in nearby Daphne, were soon called "Olympic," and though they were less regularly staged than the original Olympic Games, they rivaled in splendor those in the Peloponnesus.[27] The citizens of Antioch believed that the "Olympic Games" in Daphne were proof of their own importance and resisted attempts to end their international festival. However, the Byzantine emperor finally ended these counterfeit Olympics by decree in A.D. 520 because of violent clashes of blues and greens which broke out after a chariot race in Daphne in A.D. 507.

When the ancient festival at Olympia itself ceased cannot be ascertained, but it certainly occurred long before this last date. The antiquarian respect that led the Romans to keep some Greek festivals going did not extend to the barbarian horde called Herulians who sailed out of the Black Sea in A.D. 267. Having occupied Byzantium, Corinth, and Argos, they sacked Athens. At Olympia, the frightened Elians decided that stone from surrounding (mostly Roman) buildings should be used to build a protecting wall around the temple of Zeus and the holiest part of the altis. After this the records become scarce. In A.D. 394 Theodosius the Great stopped the reckoning of time in Olympiads and banned all pagan festivals, which would make the Olympic Games of A.D. 393—the 293d Olympics since the first recorded Games in 776 B.C.—the last to be held. Theodosius also removed the most admired artwork of ancient times—the ebony, ivory, and gold statue of the Olympian Zeus—to Byzantium where it was destroyed by fire in A.D. 476.

More barbarian invaders plundered Olympia in the fourth century. The Christianized Greeks were at this time urged to obliterate the remaining prestige of paganism by leveling the ancient holy sites. But for Olympia worse was yet to come. Earthquakes in A.D. 522 and 551 toppled the columns of the temple of Zeus and the temple of Hera. The river Alpheios changed its course, washing away all of the hippodrome and covering the rest of Olympia with layer upon layer of clay. Though Olympia and its festival lived on in the hearts of those who loved Greece, for centuries its exact location was a mystery.

2

PROPOSALS FOR REVIVAL

*O*NE MIGHT VIEW every athletic festival at Olympia after 146 B.C., the year Greece was brought into the Roman empire, as a revival. After that date, Greek sport had only loose connections with Greek religion, art, education, and pride. The Olympic Games continued because influential Romans, particularly those under the Antonines, were fond of these theatrical evocations of the superior culture which in this and other ways they preserved, absorbed, and propagated.

The Romans' recreations, especially those of the well-born and educated, were for the most part passive and vicarious. Sports epics or Pindaric odes to athletes, which were natural to the classical Greeks, were artificial for the Romans. Vergil's inclusion of athletic contests in the *Aeneid* is due to the momentum of the Homeric tradition.[1] Our loss of the many Greek manuals on athletic training is due to the lack of interest on the part of Roman readers. The Romans wrote very little on hunting or fishing, nor did they translate Greek works on the subjects. Hunting was considered a servile occupation by Sallust, a chilly one by Horace. As a noted historian has observed, "Varro's chapter on wild boars is occupied mainly with fattening them in captivity, and leads up to a chapter on fattening snails, at best a slow sport."[2]

Greek athletics were preserved in Roman culture as nostalgic theater, while church authorities in the West opposed the circuses and festivals of the Romans because they were considered the work of the devil. The sports of Christian Europe sprang anew from two separate sources. One was from the local, peasant culture in the villages and consisted of informal athletic contests usually performed as adjuncts to religious holidays and local fairs. This ancient sporting tradition, because it developed among the illiterate population, left only the most meager documentary evidence until very late in European history. The other source was to be found in aristocratic social life and grew out of hunting and practice for combat. This sporting tradition inspired art and literature.[3] The sports of the feudal nobility acquired certain traditions of their own, so that whatever the origin or racial composition of the ruling classes in Europe, their sports were for centuries remarkably similar. These sports were fiercely aggressive and ceremoniously maintained and preserved in the face of a relentlessly opposing Christian orthodoxy.

Though there was a lack of continuity in the actual forms of Greek and Roman sport on the one hand and the forms of Roman and European sport on the other, the prestige of classical culture never died. Its prestige became very great indeed in the period we call the Renaissance, especially in Italy, where Italian collectors reestablished what they believed were the canons of Greco-Roman taste in all the visual arts. To the Italian humanists we also owe the collection and preservation of almost all the classical literary texts which we now possess, including the sources from which we determine what Greek physical education and sport were like. Italian intellectuals were inspired by classical educational theorists to concoct their own schemes for an ideal education that, like the Greeks', integrated training for the mind and training for the body. Vittorino da Feltre, Guarino da Verona, Alberti, Pico della Mirandola, and others inspired later pedagogues all over Europe to include plans for physical education in their writings. These included François Rabelais, Michel Montaigne, Huldreich Zwingli, Johannes Bugenhagen, Thomas Elyot, John

Locke and Jean Jacques Rousseau.[4] These writers, in turn, inspired the reformers, philanthropists, and nationalists who established programs for physical training in many education systems in Europe in the nineteenth century.

If this period was marked by advances in theories of physical education, the broad period of the Enlightenment in Europe represented a break in the evolution of sports. The languid, artificial tone of much of the social life of the Enlightenment was partly a reaction to the stuffy pomp and the grim warfare in the Europe of Louis XIV, who died in 1715. The feudal aristocracy's compulsion to give theatrical demonstrations of physical and military prowess in combative exercise was altered. Hunting became much less an obsession. In the eighteenth century tournaments were on a smaller scale and were viewed sentimentally by both participants and spectators, much as the later Romans attended the artificially preserved Olympic Games. Good health was of course to be desired, if not pursued. Sport, violent effort, sweaty spectacle—all were antithetical to the style of gilded shell-pink or shell-blue interiors, the ease, comfort, and wit of the salons, the dancing, gambling, and intrigue of the courts. Fencing was still a gentleman's sport, but the duels tended to become rare—"grace à la philosophie," according to one philosophe.[5] A critic of the too-exquisite philosophes has noted that at this time the umbrella was invented.[6] Those who could afford it took carriages or sedan chairs rather than riding or walking. If one had to cross the Alpine passes, he drew the blinds of his stage so that the measured order of his thoughts would not be affronted by the sight of such untamed, tumultous nature.

Much of the harsh social criticism of Rousseau, particularly in his educational theories contained in the novel *Emile* (1792), should be seen against the background of aristocratic lassitude which characterized this period. Voltaire observed in a letter:

Of course, the victories in the Greek games—from the discus throw to the chariot race—were hotly contested. And to win in our own ancient

tournaments or tiltings was well worth a struggle. But today! Now all
great personages, from Petersburg to Moscow, pass their days in flabby
idleness. The sole attractions are those miserable card games. Isn't it
likely that such drowsy activities cause their souls to atrophy too?[7]

Before moving on to discuss in more detail the social and
intellectual background of the modern Olympic Games, I would
like to survey briefly the later history of the word "Olympia."
Quite naturally the name of the site and of the chronological
span based on the quadrennial appearance of the festival both
passed into Latin. The word "Olympias" appears in early
medieval Latin literature almost exclusively as a period of time,
not always four years long. Some of the early medieval emperors
tried grandly to reckon the length of their reigns in Olympiads.[8]
Early French writers also used the word in referring to periods
of time. Later authors used *olympien* allusively to suggest the
withdrawn, all-seeing gods who dwelled on Mount Olympus in
northern Greece. At least two pieces of music published in
France in the 1720s were named after the *jeux olympiques*.[9]
Voltaire, a charmed spectator at an athletic festival in England
in 1727, wrote that he felt "transporté aux jeux olympiques."[10]
Flaubert and Gide both used to word *olympique* in their
writings, but not in reference to athletic contests.[11] There was
for a while a theater called the "Cirque olympique" in Paris,
and "feu olympique" once described a fire started by concen-
trating the sun's rays with a magnifying glass or a concave
mirror.[12]

In England the word "Olympic" or something like it was most
often used to refer to athletic events. In 1592 Shakespeare
referred to "such rewards as victors weare at the Olympian
Games" in Act Two of *Henry VI* and referred to "Olympian
wrestling" in Act Four of *Troilus and Cressida*. John Milton
recalled "th' Olympian Games" in *Paradise Lost* in 1667. In the
eighteenth and nineteenth centuries, usages of "Olympia" and
its derivatives were more common in English than in other
European languages.[13] The English also appear to have devel-

oped, enjoyed, and maintained a particularly rich athletic tradition. And in keeping with the relative looseness of English society, peasant festivals and courtly tournaments were not so far apart in social appeal as they were on the continent.

In the early seventeenth century a wealthy Captain Robert Dover established on his estate in the Cotswolds an annual "Olympick Games" that took place on Thursday and Friday of Whitsun week. Dover, a Catholic, planned the gaudy celebration as a protest against the infectious puritanism of his time. For some years these "Cotswold Olympics" attracted spectators from as far away as London. The events of the festival and the ceremony accompanying them both show that the celebration, despite its name, was a harking back to the village and courtly traditions and not to the Greeks. The events consisted of "wrestling, playing cudgels, fencing, leaping, pitching the bar, throwing the iron hammer or handling the pike while the young women were dancing to the tune of a shepard's pipe."[14] A temporary "castle" was mounted on top of a pivot on a central height (still called "Dover's hill") near the playing fields. Cannons announced the opening of the games. There was revelry and feasting in the tents for the gentry. As the chief official, Dover rode about the fields on a white horse, wearing a broad-brimmed hat and a ruff.

We know about these events and the merriness that accompanied them chiefly from a book of poems published in 1636 and dedicated to Dover and his games.[15] The list of its distinguished contributors includes Ben Johnson, Michael Drayton, and Thomas Heywood. The poems compare the English games with the classical games and eulogize Dover as a second Hercules. Here is Drayton's poem:

Dover, to doe thee Right, who will not strive,
That dost in these dull yron Times revive
The golden Ages glories; which poore Wee
Had not so much as dream't on but for Thee?
As those brave Grecians in their happy dayes,

On Mount Olympus to their Hercules
Ordain'd their games Olimpik, and so nam'd
Of that great Mountaine; for those pastimes fam'd:
Where then their able Youth, Lept, Wrestled, Ran,
Threw the arm'd Dart; and honour'd was the Man
That was the Victor; in the cirkute there
The nimble Rider, and the skil'd Chariotere
Strove for the Garland; In those noble Times
There to their Harpes the Poets sang their Rimes;
That whilst Greece flourish't, and was onely then
Nurse of all Arts, and of all famous men:
Numbering their years, still their accounts they made,
Either from this or that Olympiade,
So Dover, frome these Games, by thee begun,
Wee'l reckon Ours, as time away doth run.

Dover himself answered his friends in the final poem in the book:

I cannot tell what Plannet rul'd, when I
First undertooke this Mirth, this jollitie;
Nor can I give account to you at all,
How this conceit into my braine did fall,
Or how I durst assemble, call together
Such multitudes of people as come hither.
Whilst Greece frequented active Sport and Playes,
From other men they bore away the Prayse;
Their common-Wealths did flourish; and their Men
Unmatch'd were for worth and Honour then:
But when they once those pastimes did forsake,
And unto drinking did themselves betake,
So base they grew, that at this present day
They are not men, but moving lumps of Clay. . . .[16]

What makes these charming poems interesting to the sports historian is the early use of athletic enthusiasm and sports festivities as devices to link Englishmen with the revered Greeks. The Cotswold games stopped with Robert Dover's death in 1641, but were revived briefly by Charles II. We also have evidence that elsewhere in England in the seventeenth century there were athletic festivals called "Olympics."[17]

Moving rapidly ahead to the nineteenth century, for more than forty years after the first festival in 1849 a certain Dr. W. P. Brookes staged yearly "Olympic Games" in a grassy valley near the town of Wenlock in Shropshire. There were awards for running, tilting at a ring from horseback, jumping, and cricket, as well as prizes for literary compositions and other artistic works. The pageantry included heralds with red velvet caps and white feathers, marching bands, banners of local athletic associations, and schoolchildren singing hymns and casting flower petals. The processional route was from two local taverns, the Raven and the Gaskel Arms, to the "Olympian Fields." At the awards ceremonies ladies crowned kneeling champions with laurel. There were raised banners with Greek inscriptions. Participants planted saplings which were solemnly baptized with champagne. By dedicating the trees to the Greek ministers in London and to the Greek royal house, Brookes gained the attention of the king in Athens who sent a large silver urn to be passed on to the annual victor in the pentathlon. (Our principal narrative source for these events is the French social critic, Baron Pierre de Coubertin, who noted in his report of the festival that "since ancient Greece has passed away, the Anglo-Saxon race is the only one that fully appreciates the moral influence of physical culture and gives to this branch of educational science the attention it deserves.")[18]

Spiritual bonds between the noble Greeks and Englishmen were claimed by the English themselves. There was, in fact, considerable discussion in Great Britain in the 1890s over prospects for an "Anglo-Saxon Olympiad." The leading promoter of the scheme, one J. Astley Cooper, had a problem, however, and one that would become familiar to many subsequent promoters of amateur athletics. Cooper's difficulty was not in defining "amateur," the word that still causes problems today, but in deciding who belonged to the "Anglo-Saxon race."

While his games were to include events regularly practiced by Britons, Americans, and "colonials," he conceived the festival as being for the benefit of the white and wellborn alone:

The scheme ought to act as an antidote to the debilitating effects of luxury, wealth and civilisation, for, should it be carried out in its full conception, the honors which it affords should be those for which the flower of the Race would chiefly strive. [19]

In his comments on the use of the term "Olympiad," one of Cooper's correspondents, Mr. (later Lord) George Curzon, under secretary (later viceroy) of India, wrote:

I do not in the least demur to the comparison with the Olympian Games and other Hellenic contests. It is precisely the same spirit of emulous but friendly rivalry, of absorbing popular interest, and of patriotism that you want to excite, and that should be stimulated in a far greater degree among a people of an empire that covers the globe than it ever was amid the dependencies of a small nation restricted to the Mediterranean. [20]

An inspired, patriotic American correspondent suggested "ambulatory" games alternating between Britain and the United States. Another American, ambitious for America's largest international exhibition, the imminent "World's Columbian Exposition" of 1893 in Chicago, proposed that

If this matter of an International Athletic Festival to be held every three or four years is to be taken up seriously, what more auspicious year to inaugurate it than that of our World's Fair, when the eyes of the universe are upon us. [21]

This was not the first mention of American "Olympic Games." In Congress in 1779, Representative William Henry Drayton sought approval for a display of fireworks to celebrate American independence. In his argument for fireworks, Drayton pointed out irrelevantly that the Olympic Games were used by the Greeks to celebrate the birth of their nation and that the Games "were calculated for improving bodily strength, to make men athletic and robust." Another representative, Henry Laurens, opposed this "funny declamation" and declared that "the Olympian Games and other fooleries brought on the desolation of the Greeks."[22]

Certain proposals for revivals of the Olympic Games moved beyond the discussion stages in Greece itself. One Evangelios Zappas (1800–1865), a grain dealer who made his fortune in Rumania, gave the so-called Zappeion to Athens. It is still used for exhibitions, but was intended then to be used for, among other things, athletic practice and contests. In 1858 Zappas also offered King Otto of Greece a large endowment for "the restoration of the Olympic Games, to be celebrated every four years, following the precepts of the ancient Greeks, our ancestors."[23]

Accordingly, a royal decree established an Olympic Committee which planned an athletic festival for a Sunday in November, 1859. The games took place in Place Louis, a square on the outskirts of Athens, which then had about 30,000 inhabitants. There were sprints and longer races suitably called the diaulos and dolichos, which were ancient Greek words. There were also standing and running broad jumps, and there was wrestling both standing and on the ground (clearly intended to evoke the difference in ancient times between wrestling and the pancration). Other events included the discus throw (for height as well as for distance), the high jump, rope climbing, and a team tug-of-war. The javelin was thrown at a steer's head. In addition to their olive wreaths, victors got prizes of one hundred drachmas, while the runners-up got fifty. The winner in wrestling took home a milk cow.

This evocation of the glories of ancient Greece attracted astonishingly large groups of curious and, as it turned out, disorderly onlookers. The urchins of Athens successfully evaded the police who tried to keep them back from contestants. Cavalry soldiers with sheathed swords hit at the surging spectators, including many women and small children. A contestant in the distance race expired on the spot. The presence of the king, queen, and assorted dignitaries was intended to move the onlookers to respect, but these measures failed. Enthusiastic crowds rushed the royal enclosure and had to be cleared by mounted police who, in the melee, arrested some athletes, mistaking them for disobedient subjects. There were beggars present. One high point of these Olympic Games was the appearance of a blind beggar before the king and queen to sing an ode for which he was not unrewarded. [24]

The yearned-for regularity in staging the Olympic Games could not be maintained after those of 1859, but there were further Games in 1870, 1875, and 1888. [25] For the Games of 1875, the site was the old Panathenian stadium of Herodes Atticus. It was now little more than a ravine that was provisionally tidied up and mowed. The steep sides offered good views of the contests below, but frequent quarrels on the slopes occasionally led to tussles which, in turn, produced rolling human avalanches. The running area was never free of loiterers or barking dogs who raced the athletes. The runners of the race of one stade (as in classical times, about two hundred meters) overtook a stout woman with two curs whom the officials could not remove. One dog snapped at an official who tried to chase him from the bottom of a tall greased pole at the top of which honked a fat goose. The goose was the prize for the athlete who was the first of the many who simultaneously tried to seize it. An English spectator noted that the winner "would certainly prove a dangerous neighbor in an orchard."[26]

An English observer was impressed that the judges were called "Hellenodicai" and the athletes were called "Olympioakoe," thus reverting to ancient usage. At the finish of each foot race was an official whose tail coat, white gloves, and blue silk sash identified him as a judge. The runner who got there first seized a little flag the judge held out and then danced about with the banner, waving it to the crowds who shared his joy. At the award ceremonies the winners got crowns of olive; the runners-up, branches of olive. The third-place winners received branches of oleander in flower. Some disconsolate losers were also given branches of oleander.[27] The modern Greeks were obviously inspired by the classical athletic festivals, but they lacked an established festive or ceremonial sporting tradition that was actually their own.

The classical scholars of the late nineteenth century knew a great deal about Olympia and its festivals and were able to lend their knowledge to attempts at evoking the extinct sports celebrations. As has already been emphasized, the Olympic Games were never forgotten. The prestige of the Greeks for whom the ancient Games were staged increased in modern times owing to the value placed on an education based on the classics. Another factor was the ever greater use of classical motifs, proportions, and subjects in the European arts in the eighteenth and nineteenth centuries. Neoclassicism in European taste and in European sentiment was strengthened a great deal by the published narratives and sketchbooks of travelers and scholars who visited collections of antiques and the archaeological sites. Especially influential in declaring the supremacy of Greek art were the books of illustrations and commentaries of Johann Joachim Winckelmann. This son of a cobbler, born in 1717 in Stendahl in Prussia, was able to use his knowledge and enthusiasm for classical art to achieve great fame. Although Winckelmann is sometimes called the founder of classical archaeology, his researches were done almost entirely from the few and inferior Greek monuments (e.g., at Paestum) in Italy and from the artifacts in European collections. Winckelmann was negotiating with the Turkish authorities and collecting money to locate and to dig at Olympia when he was murdered in Trieste in 1768.

The notion to seek out Olympia was, of course, not new. Several travelers in the seventeenth and eighteenth centuries tramped about the site of ancient Elis looking in vain for Olympia.[28] In August, 1766, an English theologian, Richard Chandler, with his copy of Pausanias in his hand stumbled upon a heavy wall and a huge Doric capital. This was all that could be seen of ancient Olympia which Chandler knew lay buried beneath him. A French traveler, Louis François Sebastian Fauvel, made speculative sketches of the layout of Olympia in 1787. For three days in 1806 some Englishmen engaged Turkish workers to do some digging around the temple of Zeus. Inspired by Winckelmann's speculations that Olympia would be a rich site, there were also several German projects to dig there. All were rendered useless by the Greek wars of independence which began in 1821.

Part of the large French military expedition sent to help the Greeks in 1829 was a group of scientists and scholars. Some of them went to Olympia and there engaged a hundred workers. For six weeks they excavated in the area of the temple of Zeus.[29] And, as was customary for the plundering archaeologists of the time, the French shipped some of the temple's metopes to enrich even further the collections of the Louvre. When the uncertain political conditions permitted, Olympia was increasingly a place of pilgrimage for ambitious travelers. Plans for additional, systematic excavations were frustrated, however, largely owing to the refusal on the part of the newly independent Greeks to allow the theft of more art treasures from their soil. So for several decades Olympia remained at once known and unknown. As early as 1835 a German scholar was able to write and to illustrate the first of his three volumes on Hellenic sport. These books included a lot of information about the Olympic festival.[30] But at the site itself only the base and the enormous, toppled column drums of the temple of Zeus could be seen.

Then Ernst Curtius (1814–1896)—like Winckelmann, a German classical scholar of undistinguished parentage— decided that this situation must not continue. Curtius had first seen Olympia as a twenty-four-year-old archaeology student. He advanced rapidly in German academic circles to become a professor in Berlin and a tutor to the crown prince of Prussia. In a celebrated speech before dignitaries in Berlin in 1852, Curtius said:

There lying deep in the darkness is life of our lives. It was sacred territory in a world ruled by other gods who were able to bring about peace due to the Olympic truce. But it remains holy territory for us as well. Those impulses for enchantment, that love of the fatherland, the consecration to art and the full application of energy to pursuit of joy— all these things should be offered to the clean rays of our enlightened world.[31]

One of those most impressed by the speech was Friedrich Wilhelm, the crown prince of Prussia. After the speech the prince approached Curtius and said, "One felt almost as though he himself should assume a position at the exit to shake a little box for contributions!"[32]

For some time afterward the Prussians were distracted by the diplomacy and wars which led to Germany's unification under Prussian leadership, but all the while negotiations with the Greek government progressed and financing for excavations at Olympia became more assured. The essential basis of the agreement that let the Germans go ahead was that they would pay for the excavations and that all the art discovered would remain in Greece.[33]

A series of six expeditions covering the period 1875–1881 uncovered the entire altis at Olympia. The finds of art and artifacts were not disappointing. The finest treasures, including the friezes from the temple of Zeus, can be seen in the museum (also erected by the Germans) presently near the site at Olympia. All the work and the discoveries were described in the huge, meticulously detailed official reports that were published between 1890 and 1897 in Berlin, the capital of the new German empire. Since the middle of the nineteenth century, the Germans have claimed Olympia as sentimentally and peculiarly theirs, and each series of major excavations has been used to enhance the prestige of whatever government resided in Berlin.[34] Not unexpectedly, Ernst Curtius and other Germans made wistful public statements suggesting that a suitable undertaking for the intellectuals and educationalists of their age might be a revival of the Olympic Games.

At least partly due to the identification of the Germans with Olympia, the volume and detail of scholarship on classical sport has until very recently been almost overwhelmingly the work of German academics.[35] But even apart from Olympia and German scholarship in classical sport, German artists and intellectuals have often been tempted to view themselves and their vigorous culture as possible reincarnations of the Hellenic titans and *their* culture.[36] The discoveries at Olympia merely gave the German attachment to the Greeks another sentimental dimension.

It will be necessary to touch upon several aspects of nineteenth-century sport later on, but now I would like to describe briefly some distinctive developments in German physical education. Unlike the development of sport in the Anglo-Saxon world, which grew more or less naturally and without the prodding or attention of intellectuals, German sport has always been promoted by particular persons or institutions for special (usually nationalistic and/or political) purposes. It should be pointed out here also that "sport" in this context is not sport as we think of it today. In fact, sport really ought to be considered an Anglo-Saxon invention only adopted by continentals late in the nineteenth century. Until then few Germans knew what "sport" was except from what they picked up in polemics. The Germans knew only "turning."[37]

The turning movement had its origins in the 1770s with the devising and publishing of analytical exercises intended for the advancement of children's health. These were produced by several German pedagogues, the most influential of whom was Johann C. F. Guts Muths (1759–1839).[38] For decades the development of turning was confined to quasi-scientific experiments in human movement and projects to integrate these exercises into popular education. The inspired propagator of turning (and inventor of the word *turnen*) was Friedrich Ludwig "Turnvater" Jahn (1778–1852). He established playgrounds (*Turnplätze*) and festivals (*Turntäge*). Under Jahn's leadership turning became a movement (*Turnbewegung*) for inspiring young men and for making them fit. The movement and the turners played major roles in the organized resentment against Napoleon's occupation of Germany and then in the revolutionary pressure to bring about German national unity. In these decades of imposed political stability in central Europe, the turners' movement was one of the few expressions of community and patriotic solidarity available to the restless Germans. Jahn's movement grew in appeal and became established in the minds of its bourgeois ideologues, its lower bourgeois participants, and its aristocratic enemies as an institution and a complex of attitudes that were paramilitary and conducive to democratic agitation.

The yearning of Jahn and of other patriots to bring about German independence and unity from below were hampered at first by spies and conservatives led by Prince Metternich, and then by the bungling of the German liberal nationalists. Later, bourgeois and lower-class patriots were allowed to cheer as Germany was finally united through the genius of Bismarck and the might of the Prussian armies in the decade following 1861.

As Germany consolidated her political position with rapid economic advances in the last decades of the nineteenth century, the turners were no longer seen as potentially disrupting. Scientific, artificial, disciplined exercise had been integrated into the various German systems of universal education. The clubs of the turners became focuses for local social life, while the ever larger national turners' meetings became occasions for mass demonstrations of loyalty to the united and prosperous Second Reich.

In the many writings of Guts Muths, "Turnvater" Jahn, and other German educational theorists there are suggestions that the Olympic Games might well be staged again. Several German classicists also suggested that it would be noble to revive in some way the Olympic festival. These suggestions were, however, just wistful trial balloons· and demonstrate only that in Germany, as in other parts of Europe, nostalgia for the Olympic Games was widespread, though confined to intellectuals.[39] Furthermore, the turners, who were led by narrowly patriotic, bourgeois functionaries, and the polyglot academics, who were isolated in their institutes, operated in completely different spheres of the rigidly compartmentalized society of their day. Nor did either the turners or the scholars have many contacts with like-minded people outside Germany.

Some cosmopolitan Germans, of course, were well informed about the rather different progress of physical education and, especially, of popular recreation in England. These developments, which, like turning, had their origins in the eighteenth century, had become part of English life and consciousness without the help or notice of ideologues or officials.[40] The English leisured classes had games like hockey and their two kinds of football, rowing, boxing, horse racing, and all sorts of footraces and field events. In fact many observers of the British sporting scene in the eighteenth and nineteenth centuries were struck by the fact that, as in ancient Greece, noblemen might participate in agonistic competition with commoners, and that there existed in England, as in ancient Greece, the athletic hero. It was also well known that a taste for Anglo-Saxon sporting events had become well established in America, Canada, and Australia. German critics of the artificiality and rigidity of German physical education proposed that their countrymen at least examine these appealing exercises, competitions, and games which were called "sport." The turners, however, claimed that sport was an alien infection that might damage the integral structure of robust German culture.

Although eager to enrich and to depoliticize German physical education and popular recreation, the few German defenders of sport played very small roles in the growth of international cooperation and exchange which affected all aspects of European intellectual, social, and political life in the last half of the nineteenth century. The beginning of this internationalism might be dated from the opening in May, 1851, of the Crystal Palace Exhibition. Secure, confident Great Britain invited all the nations and their colonies to display the best of their arts and industries in London that year. This, the first world's fair, demonstrated that competition between peoples could be peaceful and progressive. Subsequent international exhibitions soon surpassed the London exhibition of 1851 in numbers of visitors, numbers of exhibitors, and variety of things displayed. Beginning with the "Universal, International Exposition of 1867" in Paris, the ever larger and more frequent world's fairs became convenient meeting places for the world's traders, artists, and scholars. Exhibitions of industrial products or works of art were awarded gold, silver, or bronze medals and lavishly printed certificates of merit testifying to their superiority in international competition.

After 1870, innovations and grandeur in the world's fairs were expected mostly of those that took place in Paris. The lavishness of the French world's fairs can be seen as compensation for France's diplomatic isolation and relative economic stagnation. The Paris exposition of 1878 was the first to add international congresses for such diverse specialists as dentists, historians, and statisticians. This exposition attracted a total of 16 million visitors, more than twice that of 1867. The Paris exposition of 1889 attracted 40 million visitors. The plans for the Paris exposition of 1900 were for a cultural manifestation to be more grandly embracing than any that had preceded it. This vast display would occupy much of the center of Paris and would attract 100 million people, a figure more than twice as large as the population of France. The French confidently expected that almost every prominent person in the world would visit Paris to witness so dazzling a spectacle.[41] There would be international assemblies of every kind, including congresses for bibliographers, coin collectors, photographers, hypnotists, and beekeepers. The organizers in Paris were also preparing for a congress of physical educationalists.

Internationalism became more evident and gained more dedicated support in the later nineteenth century. A German priest launched a synthetic international language, Volapuk, which in the 1880s was supplanted by Esperanto—itself the subject for a planned international congress in Paris in 1900. The Universal Postal Union was established in 1875. There was a convention to standardize patent laws in 1883 and one for uniform copyright laws in 1887. The first Hague Peace Conference held in the summer of 1899 was unprovoked by a war and provided for the establishment of a Permanent Court of International Justice and (unsuccessfully, as it turned out) for the voluntary limitation of armaments. Long-distance travel was no longer an indulgence of the leisured rich. The network of fast trains and steamships that covered most of the civilized world also facilitated travel by the bourgeoisie who were usually pressed for time. In 1900 the crack passenger liner of the Hamburg-America Line, the Deutschland, crossed the Atlantic in just five days and seventeen hours.

In view of the internationalism that was coordinating and improving so many aspects of bourgeois intellectual life in the later nineteenth century, it must seem odd that this cosmopolitanism came so late to sport. As a partial explanation we should remember the lower bourgeois directors of the turning movement and their defense of turning's *volkisch*-patriotic ideology. A similar observation could be made about gymnastics and physical education as they developed in Scandinavia and elsewhere.[42] Thus for decades it appeared that international sporting contacts and competition were only possible among the geographically disparate but culturally homogeneous Anglo-Saxons, who were relatively uninhibited by ideology.

The English had successfully implanted their sports in the colonies. Considering the slowness of communication in the early nineteenth century, the similarities in English sport on the one hand and American, Canadian, and Australian sport on the other are astonishing.[43] Yet practice and competition all over the Anglo-Saxon world remained, with the exceptions of horse racing and distance racing and possibly cricket, remarkably localized for decades. Then, beginning in the 1850s, the codification of rules (misnamed by some sports historians as the "inventions" of various games), the standardization of events, and better transport made interregional competitions possible. Public enthusiasm, particularly, made standardization desirable.[44] The first professional, traveling baseball teams were established in the 1860s. By this time intercollegiate football games were common in the eastern United States and rugby matches were being played in the area around London. The first "international" football (soccer) match took place in Edinburgh on March 27, 1871, between teams representing England and Scotland.

The first intercollegiate track meet was held on Christ Church Ground, Oxford, on March 5, 1864, between teams from Oxford and Cambridge. The events included a 440-yard run, a mile run, hurdles of 120 and 200 yards, a steeplechase, the high jump, and the long jump. American colleges began to have track meets soon afterward. In 1875 Harvard, Yale, Princeton, Cornell, Columbia, Pennsylvania, Williams, Amherst, and Union had a very large meet which led shortly afterward to the formation of the Intercollegiate Association of Amateur Athletes of America. From approximately this time we can date the determined quest on the part of Americans and Englishmen for sports records, which were made possible partly by the availability of reliable, cheap stopwatches.

In the first truly international track meet a team from the London Athletic Club confronted a team from the New York Athletic Club at Manhattan Field in New York on September 21, 1895. The footraces ranged from the 100-yard dash to a run of three miles. There were also 120-yard hurdles, the high jump, the long jump, the shot put, and the hammer throw. Performing before a large crowd, the Americans won all eleven events. Since the occasion was reported in newspapers on both sides of the Atlantic, plans were begun immediately for a rematch.

In academic sports historiography one finds this track meet, a couple of regattas in Europe, some fencing matches, and the first modern Olympic Games all appearing rather abruptly as international sports events in the middle 1890s. This rather belated arrival of internationalism on the sport scene would seem less sudden if the historians would consider professional sport, which was international much earlier. Certain professional distance runners regularly sought out competition on both sides of the Atlantic in the mid-nineteenth century. The creation of a new sort of sports hero was made possible in the course of the rapid perfection of the "standard" bicycle during the period 1890–1894. Improvements in the racing cycle tended to occur first in France and it was in Paris that American or British stars were likely to attract the most enthusiastic crowds and, therefore, the largest purses.

Further developments which encouraged international sporting contests were the rise of a sporting press, full-time international correspondents, and the worldwide wire services. Sports journals and sports journalists had appeared early in England and later in America. Sports newspapers and, even more, sports sections in general newspapers and magazines became circulation-building enterprises in France, Belgium, and Italy, beginning about 1890. It is likely that the especially rapid development of spectator sport in the 1890s may have been further stimulated by a symbiotic relationship between news-seeking journalists and a sports-hungry reading public.

As background material, it should be noted that Anglo-Saxon sport, particularly in the 1880s, became steadily more earnest and performance-oriented. By this I mean that both the participants and their public became more obsessed with victory in local competitions and with the setting of records in regional and international competition. The results of games and contests were seen as symbolic indications of the status of the larger social unity represented by the athletes, but perhaps this is indicative only of major ideological trends or even of mass opinion in an increasingly accomplishment-oriented society. Then, too, games like cricket, intercollegiate American football, and professional baseball acquired formulas, rituals, theatrical settings, and mythic pasts that made a game with its attendant spectators reminiscent of cult celebrations in ancient and in not so ancient times.

The performance orientation in turn led to the production of better equipment. The rapid evolution of the racing bicycle has been noted. There were also lighter tennis rackets and track shoes, shorter running trousers, and more clinging bathing suits. Training became more intense, and this dedication to sporting methodology led to a vast increase in the publication of more or less scientific literature on the subject. New gymnasiums, stadiums, and amphitheaters were built to accommodate the paying sports consumers. Money from sports events made fortunes for many promoters, some gamblers, and a few athletes.

Along with the success of vulgar spectator sport and the aura of lucre surrounding it, professional sport was dreaded as corrosive to what had been, for only a slightly longer period, a preserve of the leisured rich. The rich rejected money as a reward for sporting supremacy. A campaign to preserve an area of "clean" competition apart from and above the working-class professionals dates from the mid-nineteenth century in England, and it began among the rowers. Later, the success of professional sport intensified the campaign to isolate it. In the *Nation* (New York) in 1893 a writer viewed with alarm the "athletic craze" in American universities. The promoters in the colleges were "debauching" youth by "being easy with these young professionals on examinations" and by allowing professional athletes to haunt the college buildings as sham students. But the same moralist also noted that Yale's gate receipts for intercollegiate football games more than covered the expenses for Yale's entire athletic program.[45]

At this stage I would like to summarize some of the points that have been made so far. I have discussed the uses and spread of the word "Olympia," the survival of literary records of the ancient Olympic festival, and the excavations following the rediscovery of the ancient site. I have shown that there have been many projects, both proposed and realized, to institute modern "Olympic Games." In the later nineteenth century the isolated Athenians participated in a series of sporting meets that were inspired by the myth that modern Greeks are the sole legitimate heirs of the classical Hellenes. England was the only European nation where the medieval peasant recreations and the aristocratic tournaments never perished, and, in fact, served as the foundations of modern sport. In England there were "Olympic" sports festivals as early as the seventeenth century. Later English "Olympics" recalled the sentimental and the racial traditions of ancient Greeks.

An ideologically inspired and somewhat different tradition in physical education and recreation was established in Germany in the late eighteenth century. Later the turners had their own sports festivals. Classical sport came to be considered a special province of German scholars because of their innovative work in sports historiography and, later, because of the excavations of German archaeologists at the ancient site of Olympia. In German society the classicists were separated from the turners, who, in turn, deliberately isolated themselves from Anglo-Saxon sport, which was becoming increasingly popular and widely known. The spread of sport was one aspect of the social and cultural internationalism of the late nineteenth century.

The internationalism of ideas was boosted by improvements in transportation and communication, which encouraged the first international sporting meets. Indeed, by the end of the century there were proposals to include physical education and recreation in the universal, international expositions which summarized the knowledge of the age. Though these world fairs took place all over the globe, by the last quarter of the nineteenth century it was generally accepted that the grandest ones would be staged in Paris.

In the later nineteenth century there were many proposals for international sporting meets, and proposals as well for festivals that would be called "Olympic Games." The modern Greeks felt that the "Olympics" should be uniquely theirs. The English proposals would have included many events that bore some comparisons with those in the ancient festivals. Wistful proposals came from many Germans. The driving force for modern Olympic Games, however, came from none of the above countries, but from a citizen of a nation that was generally recognized, even by its own people, as being the least athletic of all.

3

COUBERTIN

*H*IS MUSTACHE WAS splendid. It was carefully pruned, with sumptuous tendrils that swooped out to wisps at the end, beyond the width of his canted ears and broad, asymmetrical forehead. He looked like a whiskered cat destined for a long life. When Pierre de Coubertin was young and full of projects, his dense, waving hair was jet black. These were the years when this aristocratic defender of the Third Republic was a historian, a journalist, a social critic, and the proselytizer of sport to his nation. Much later, when Coubertin was a living monument and a lonely deviser of projects for educational reform, his hair turned gray and then white. When he was aged, and hairy facial displays were no longer in fashion, the mustache, also white, drooped downward, but it still characterized the venerable, lined face. His heavy eyebrows and piercing eyes were always dark. In fact, his eyes were so dark as to appear to be without pupils. They were a bit popped, with Italian verve. Coubertin was infectiously vivacious and moved rapidly like a muscled panther, but it was mostly his eyes that stayed fixed in the memories of all who knew him. Dazzling and aggressive, they were the eyes of a man continually gauging the possibilities for action, assessing the nature of the present in order subtly to form the future. They were the eyes of a minor prophet.

Pierre de Coubertin was unusually small. We can be sure that his stature was on *his* mind, but few remained conscious of his size after the first meeting. He was big in energy, lucid in speech, and gloriously expansive in projects. There was no eccentricity or even compromise in his costume. An aura of physical euphoria, or at least good health, hovered over Pierre and, rather curiously, complemented his cravats, frock coats, striped trousers, and high, polished shoes. On first meeting this man with a peppy organ-grinder's good looks, one expected to find a rich sense of humor. Everyone soon learned that this was not so. His verve and imagination, as perhaps must be the case with a man who pursues large projects almost alone, were revealed in irony that was light and cynical when he was young and became more bitter and sad as the decades passed. Pierre de Coubertin was very serious.

He was born on New Year's Day, 1863, in the family hotel at 20 rue Oudinot in Paris. Behind the town house's four-story facade was a courtyard with neat gardens. There were spacious salons, with furniture from the ateliers of the *grands ébénistes*, art objects, big paintings, and rows of leather-bound, gilt-trimmed books. Pierre's family traced its origin to a family of Roman citizens, the de Fredis. One ancestor, Felici de Fredis, discovered the Hellenistic sculpture group, "The Laocoön," and gave it to Pope Leo X in 1506. [1] A branch of this important family had moved to France at the end of the fifteenth century to serve the kings of France. Pierre de Frédy (to use the French version of the Italian name) was Chamberlain of Louis XI, who ennobled him and gave him a coat of arms in 1477. For centuries thereafter Pierre de Frédy's descendants managed to maintain one or more members of the family close to the summit of French power. One Jean de Frédy acquired the estate of Coubertin at Saint Rémy-les-Chevreuse, near Versailles, in 1577. His great-grandson, François de Frédy, a naval officer under Louis XIV and Louis XV, had a chateau built on the property at the beginning of the eighteenth century. Soon afterward, some members of the family took their particled name from the estate rather than from their remote Italian forebears.

The Frédy-Coubertins continued to serve France as army

officers, lawyers, and judges in the courts of the nobility. During the Revolution the most prominent member of the family wisely consented to be addressed simply as "Citizen" Frédy-Coubertin and survived the tumult unmolested. However, a near relation, Henri Louis de Frédy, was beheaded at the age of 73. In 1822 the restored Bourbon monarch, Louis XVIII, awarded Julien Bonaventure, a son of the "citizen," the title of Baron de Frédy. Julien Bonaventure had married Caroline de Pardieu, whose family traced its lineage back to the early Crusaders. Their son, Charles-Louis, Baron Frédy de Coubertin, born in 1822, was the father of Pierre. Pierre's mother, born Agathe Gabrielle de Grisenoy de Mirville, was also of an ancient noble family. With her marriage, Agathe added to the Coubertin properties a chateau at Mirville near Bolbec in Normandy.

We could have ignored this genealogy were it not the case that the weight of a distinguished ancestry fell heavily on young Pierre de Coubertin. His parents made no effort to suppress their disgust for Louis Napoleon (later Napoleon III). They and their intimates ignored the Bonapartist Second Empire of the 1850s and 1860s and the insecure Third Republic that followed it. An article of their faith was that the Bourbon line would return to the throne of France.

Baron Charles-Louis regularly painted large tableaux which depicted dramatic moments in ancient French history or which glorified the papacy. The central attraction of one hall in the Paris mansion was a huge canvas of that early Italian Fredis offering "The Laocoön" to Leo X. Charles-Louis's "Le cortège pontifical" won a prize in the Salon of 1861 and Napoleon III, oblivious of the artist's contempt for him, purchased "La promenade d'un cardinal romain."[2] Charles-Louis's murals also decorated churches, and many of his paintings are still on view in provincial public galleries in France. Agathe was yet more pious than her husband. She surrounded the children with chalices, triptychs, and tapestries of annunciations and the agonies of martyrs. Pierre's mother was devoted to the idea of Christian charity and impressed upon her four children the notions of noblesse oblige. When she was in the country, she took medicine to the sick.

When Pierre was a child, the family was close and affectionate. They walked in the parks of Paris or in the French countryside. Pierre had access to the well-groomed horses of the family stables. His airy room in the Paris hotel had a rocking chair and a piano. English sporting prints were on the walls and there was a shaggy, polar bear rug on the floor.

Each year the baron and baroness, with Paul, Albert, Pierre, and Marie (born in that order), journeyed to Rome in the family's horse-drawn coach, stopping along the way for stately, though friendly, visits in chateaux or castellos having marble salons and formal gardens with fountains and clean, graveled walks. The *Almanach de Gotha* was a domestic reference book. Each year the whole family solemnly observed the birthday of the Bourbon claimant to the French throne, the aging, exiled Count of Chambord, called "Henry V." In 1879, when Pierre was sixteen, the family was received by this stubborn, dying "king" at his isolated residence in Frohsdorf in the Austrian Tyrol.[3] He had been in exile for fifty years.

Pierre's father was one of the handsomest men of his age. He was tall, with a long nose and widely separated, light blue eyes. He had a full beard that was short and brushed with a central part, emphasizing the languid symmetry of his Nordic face. Paul, the oldest son, was blessed with a refined intelligence and a gift for poetry that, for a while, would make him a darling of the best salons in Paris. Albert resembled his father in his looks and attitudes, but he was interested in a military career. Marie, the youngest, was sweet-tempered and played the harp.

Pierre, born third, resembled the others in the family hardly at all. He was a slightly runted, hyperactive mesomorph. His nose was off center and he had an ever so slightly drooped left eyelid. He was almost swarthy and looked like a genetic throwback to remote Ligurian forebears. Though affectionate, he was unpredictably rebellious. When they were all in the country, Pierre's behavior was not so condescending and decorous as that of the rest of the family. He rode horses hard and fraternized with the peasants. At the age of twelve, he horrified his parents by stating in the presence of a visitor that the radical republican, Léon Gambetta, was a true French patriot. Shortly after the triumphant family audience with "Henry V" in 1879, Pierre learned that an uncle of his mother, an abbé, had been a faithful disciple of the priest Felicité Robert de Lamennais (1782–1854), whom the ultra-Catholics accused of socialism and free thought. The family burned all the granduncle's works and portraits and fasted on the anniversary of his birth, October 30. When Pierre suggested that a mass be held instead, there was an uproar. A painful break in his close ties with his mother came when she learned that he had located the uncle's sarcophagus, weed-ridden and devoid of Christian symbols, near the summer home in Mirville. The objective of Pierre's long rides on his mount had been this site, which he cleared and decorated with flowers.

As was expected of him, Pierre took fencing lessons. He took up rowing in an individual scull—at the time almost exclusively an English sport. Surreptitiously, he also practiced boxing, which was not only emphatically English but which reeked of lower-class brawling as well. Possibly some of Pierre's athleticism was attributable to his rebelliousness, although he always avoided confrontations with his family and with his social peers.

The parents sent the boy to a Jesuit lycée on the rue de Madrid in Paris, where he was remembered as a docile, intelligent pupil who showed a particular attachment to the priest who taught rhetoric. He received his baccalaureate at the age of seventeen in 1880. He was rich, well-mannered, and titled. If he lacked conventional good looks, his good taste and animation more than compensated.

Before moving on to discuss Pierre de Coubertin's accomplishments, it is necessary to review briefly a series of political events that deeply disturbed the Coubertins and, for that matter, all of Europe at the time. I refer to the calamitous defeat of France by Prussia in the war of August and September, 1870, the subsequent upheavals of the Commune, and the uncertain foundations of the French Third Republic thereafter. These were years of political humiliation and indecision during which many French patriots learned to acknowledge with agony that France, which had long been universally recognized as the world's most civilized and powerful nation, no longer had a claim to this position.

Over all of France's humiliations loomed the almost unmentionable specter of Germany, as personified by the Chancellor of the Empire, Otto von Bismarck. After 1870 the grand decisions in balance-of-power politics were made in Berlin. Germany's scientists, technicians, and salesmen helped her manufacturers sell German chemicals, electrical equipment, and banking and shipping services. Though Germany's internal transportation system was formed late, the network grew rapidly and benefited from later technological discoveries. Like Great Britain before her, Germany led the Industrial Revolution after 1870. Exports boomed. Of all the Europeans, the Germans became the best breeders; Frenchmen were the worst. This is important because an expanding population is a younger population—a demographic fact with military implications that Frenchmen regarded with horror. German music, philosophy, social thought, and even literature made further inroads into French self-confidence.[4] The new Germans were industrious, loyal, and rich. And they had the best educational system in the world.

These widely observed changes in European politics and high culture had their effect on young Pierre de Coubertin. His childhood was spent in a milieu of detestation for the illegitimate and doomed (everyone knew it) Bonapartist regime. In the 1870s, when the Republic was still insecure, the boy debated with the Jesuits about the wisest political course for France. He

later recalled his shame at the "disparate effigies" on the coins
in his pocket, the "repeated disorders" and "ridiculous insta-
bility" of his fatherland's history.[5] By the year 1880, Pierre had
become one of the few of the old aristocracy to acknowledge that
the patriotism of aggressive republicans such as Gambetta and
Jules Simon was as pure and as noble as his own. He felt that
France, if necessary a republican France, must again be grand
and powerful and therefore worthy of his vigorous devotion.

To the very bravest of the French, those tough enough to
examine the German phenomenon, it was clear that the modern
Germans could instruct the French, especially in the philosophy and techniques of her wide-reaching public education
system. If military security, territorial expansion, social stability, and national wealth were worthwhile goals, it might have
been obvious (especially to those Frenchmen who viewed the
preparation of youth as crucial for the strength of the nation)
that some aspects of imperial Germany might be dispassionately
examined and, conceivably, imitated.

Young Pierre de Coubertin searching for ideals to which he
could devote his energies and wealth, was not one of the braver
French social critics in the early 1880s. To look to France's
eastern neighbor, the land of Bismarck, was not only difficult to
consider, but, had he done so, it would have rendered him a
puzzle, perhaps even a threat, to the literary, salon-attending,
banqueting (and anti-German) society he moved in. He chose,
instead, to learn from the example of England.

Anglophilia was not new to the French, particularly to French
intellectuals. In the eighteenth century Voltaire's espousal of
Locke's philosophy determined much of the tone of the French
Enlightenment. Montesquieu sojourned in England, and his
admiration of English character and politics was evident in his
Esprit des lois (1748), a basic text for subsequent French
political critics and reformers. The industrial transformation of
Western society had begun in England. English gold played a
large role in defeating Napoleonic France. French liberals were

painfully aware that Great Britain, unlike France, proceeded without revolution to give ever larger numbers of Englishmen a voice in internal political affairs. After 1837, throughout the rest of the century, only one face, the slowly puffing one of Victoria, appeared on British coins. English technology, industry, literature, and social thought were original, vigorous, and widely disseminated. The British Empire grew to cover much of the world. And in Pierre's youth his peers had already adopted English words ("smoking," "weekend," "jockey," "club"), English tweeds, English racehorses, and English hunting dogs. Until 1870, the nineteenth century for Britain could be seen as a series of unequaled triumphs. The glories of France, on the other hand, seemed confined to the past. Thus it was time to examine France's errors and correct them.

As Germany's rise had been grudgingly attributed to her educational system, so Pierre de Coubertin determined that England's successes might also be attributable to the English system of education. Now a perceptive description of certain aspects of English education was available in the analytical travel reminiscences of that titan of French intellectual life, the politically conservative Hippolyte Taine (1828–1893). Coubertin devoured Taine's chapter on education in his *Notes sur Angleterre* (based upon visits in 1859 and 1862 and first published in France in 1872) which dealt with the English "public" (i.e., private) secondary schools. In it Coubertin read:

Whereas, with us, adolescence is spent, as it were, under a *cloche* of artificiality, through which penetrates the moral and physical reek of a great city, here [in England] it is spent in the open air, without any kind of sequestration, the boys going free in the fields, waters, and woods.

[The English pupils must put in a] maximum of eight hours work a day; it is more likely to be six or seven. With us it is eleven, which is unreasonable. An adolescent needs physical exercises: it is against nature to force him to be all brain, a sedentary bookworm. Here [in the public schools], athletic games, fives, football, running, rowing and, above all, cricket take up a part of every day. . . . Pride plays an important part; each school tries to beat its rivals and sends teams of players and oarsmen, picked out and trained, to play and row against the others.

And there are, in point of fact, gentlemen in this country whose ambition and regimen are those of a Greek athlete; they adopt a special diet, abstain from all excesses of eating and drinking. . . . I have been told of a team of eleven cricketeers who actually went to play in Australia, as formerly athletes went from Punt or Marseille, to Olympia.

Taine went on to suggest that the hierarchical organization and team sports of the English preparatory schools and the universities bred a spirit of respectful association and was an "apprenticeship in both obedience and command." Consequently, unlike French scholars who upon leaving school were likely to conclude that rules are absurd and authority contemptible, Englishmen "reconcile liberty and subordination [and they] are nearer to an understanding of the conditions in which the society can exist and the rights and duties of a citizen."[6]

Taine acknowledged that this particular kind of education was about five times the cost per pupil as that for a good classical education in France, and that, consequently, only a small minority of the population had access to it. But Coubertin passed quickly over these and other disagreeable points. He sought out a book that Taine mentioned several times, a novel that described the atmosphere of the English schools, Thomas Hughes's *Tom Brown's School Days* (first published in England in 1857 as *Tom Brown's School Days at Rugby by an Old Boy*). Pierre had read it as a boy but he remembered only anecdotes. It had appeared in installments in the *Journal de la jeunesse* in 1875 and was later published as *Les années de collège de Tom Brown*. As a questing young man, Pierre re-read Thomas Hughes. This time, however, he read as Nietzsche read Schopenhauer, as one reads perhaps once in a lifetime: to further the formation of a philosophy.[7]

Written in a nostalgic haze by a former pupil at Rugby, *Tom Brown's School Days* describes the family troubles, studies, floggings, pranks, fights, and, most especially, the athletics and games of a fictionalized pupil, the son of a country squire. *Tom Brown's School Days* is about Rugby during the reign of its celebrated headmaster, Thomas Arnold. It has intricate plotting, appealing youthful characters, an attractive natural setting, and lots of suspenseful adventure. Over sixty editions were published in its first six years and upon this single book was founded the great publishing firm of Macmillan, then in its shaky infancy.

A gently suspicious reading of an early edition of *Tom Brown's School Days* (later editions were altered usually to lessen the bloodshed) makes it seem curious that it could captivate a normally critical adult. The intention is too patently to elevate the honest, the Christian, the healthy, and the noble. It is altogether too "jolly." The good boys are inevitably small and handsome, the evil ones large and ugly. The fistfights—and there are many (Coubertin liked this)—are won by the underdogs. This influential book painted a stimulating, lively picture of the institutionalized supremacy of the upper-form boys with their "fags" in the lower forms doing the traditional, menial tasks. Hughes did not, of course, even hint at the psychologically crippling sexuality that goes along with "fagging" (the first-formers are, after all, merely children). Hughes also praises the wise natural order that supposedly results by permitting the boys freely to form their own society, a society whose abuses are checked from above by flogging, which was unheard of in France. Fresh from the relentlessly intellectual atmosphere of the Jesuit lycée, Pierre ate up *Tom Brown*. Here at last was an explanation of England's supremacy and France's degeneracy; here Pierre could see his own athletic spontaneity praised and depicted as a constructive force.

In Coubertin's France, each lycée reinforced minutely-refined divisions of the wealthy and privileged according to regional, political, and historical loyalties. In the English schools there was supposedly a rough equality among aristocratic and upper-middle-class boys. Though young Coubertin was hardly a democrat, he would have gone along with the Napoleonic slogan, "La carrière ouverte aux talents."

Tom Brown's hero, and, as it turned out, the lifelong hero of Coubertin, was the charismatic, adored Thomas Arnold, D.D., "The Doctor" as he is called in the novel. "The Doctor" is a father figure: warm, tender, and stern, though just. He follows the athletic activities of his beloved boys, though he does not referee or participate. Arnold was in fact revered by some pupils during his lifetime and legends grew about him shortly after his death at Rugby in 1848 at the early age of 47. Later, he was widely credited with being a dauntless crusader for all kinds of curriculum changes in the upper-class preparatory schools. However, as a later biographer of Arnold has pointed out, his reputation as a reformer was not deserved:

Unfortunately for the legend, the reforms which we now regard as most worthwhile—the reduction of flogging, courtesy instead of brutality among the boys, the disappearance of classical rickets in a widening of the curriculum—had nothing to do with Arnold; while his own particular insistence on the clergyman-master as a curator of souls, the powers of the flogging Sixth and an intense religious attitude among the boys, have gone altogether.[8]

During the fifteen years of his headmastership, Arnold did increase the enrollment and improve the finances of Rugby, but his zeal was much more directed at the supposedly deteriorating English moral and political conditions than to the management of Rugby. Although he urged extensions of the franchise, he was no democrat. His obsessive fears of a mass uprising of the evil poor, whom he feared and loathed (as did most of the British upper classes), may have hastened his early death. He became bogged down in discrediting, widely publicized lawsuits (one was over excessive, unjust flogging), and he had miserable relations with the townspeople of Rugby. He stayed aloof from his students, except for his sixth formers, whom he depended upon to maintain order. His extended vacations and unauthorized absences were a scandal. Although Arnold was an avid walker, runner, and horseman, he viewed these activities as entirely apart from his work. He wanted the boys to be Christians, gentlemen, and educated persons—in that order. In all his writings, he took the position of a staunch traditionalist, a man rigid in his prescribed morality, an irascible hater of his own times and a pessimist about the future. The study of Herodotus and Thucydides and the rhetorical defense of the Anglican church against its enemies were his most sincere intellectual pursuits. [9] In his celebrated biographical sketch of Arnold in *Eminent Victorians* (1918), Lytton Strachey suggested that Arnold was a neurasthenic prig. [10] Thus Coubertin's notion of Arnold and of Arnold's contribution to certain aspects of British education, particularly physical education, was a consciously created myth inspired by a writer of children's books. Coubertin's further embellished Arnold was a wise scholar and a genial coach who single-handedly established an English curriculum that was uniquely suited to the practicalities of modern life. To Coubertin, Arnold's program integrated intellectual discipline with athletic activities, and the emphasis on team sports, especially, helped to form British character. This was what Coubertin called *"le régime arnoldien."*

For a while after he left the lycée Pierre considered entering Saint-Cyr to become an army officer like his brother Albert. He attended lectures at the University of Paris by Albert Sorel and Anatole Leroy-Beaulieu. He used his family's considerable prestige and his own lively charm to move in Parisian high society. He frequented the salons and recherché receptions of the Princesse de Sagan and the Comtesse de Luynes. He practiced with the epée in the company of other aristocratic youths. He regularly rode, rowed, and boxed. As he led this delicious life—a favored man, in a favored place, in a favored epoch—he brooded on the question, "What should I do?"

He would put off a decision as he traveled. In 1883 he left for England. His parents were frightened, for were not those people enemies of Jean d'Arc and the French armies at Blenheim? Were they not all Protestants? To soothe his family, Pierre promised he would call at Sheen House in London, the residence of the then "legitimate" heir to the French throne, "His Royal Highness" the Count of Paris.[11] Once in England, Pierre became a hanger-on at the more prestigious universities and schools. He liked to hobnob, dine, and drink at Oxford and Cambridge. At the spacious green campuses of the ancient preparatory schools, he was oddly exultant when he saw notice-filled bulletin boards, cricket matches, and floggings. Once he looked on with great interest as a "fag" of aristocratic lineage massaged the sweaty, naked torso of an acquaintance of Coubertin, an upper-form athlete who was the son of a prosperous grocer.[12] Pierre's title and some letters of introduction from Paris gave him access to such political figures as William Gladstone and Austen Chamberlain. In 1886 began the copious flow of Coubertin's articles, published speeches, and books analyzing English social life and praising the English upper classes, all of which were really intended to alert Frenchmen to the decadence of their nation.

A great deal of his writing began to dwell on the methodology of physical education. Establishing himself as an expert in physical education, he sought out high-ranking bureaucrats in the Third Republic, and he embarked on a campaign to gather the control of French amateur athletics (such as they were) into his own hands. Coubertin established international connections with a questionnaire on "balance" in higher education abroad. This inquiry he sent to secondary schools in the British Empire and to ninety schools in the United States. His responses showed that the Anglo-Saxons generally favored some combination of physical and intellectual effort. For Pierre de Coubertin this was evidence of the appeal and usefulness of "le régime arnoldien."

In the summer of 1889 Coubertin left for the United States. His official task was to investigate innovations in American high schools and colleges for the Ministry of Education in Paris. He was an energetic tourist. [13] At a "Physical Training Conference" in Boston in the autumn of 1889 Coubertin was most impressed to observe that two thousand men assembled at four sessions to hear thirty-four papers. He himself spoke. It must have been odd for these Americans to hear a French baron laud the English schools, the sublime excellence of which Coubertin attributed to Thomas Arnold, "the greatest of modern teachers." Coubertin also met Theodore Roosevelt, who became one of his lifelong heroes. He visited Canada. The proximate, coexisting English-speaking and French-speaking systems permitted him to draw comparisons, and the French Anglophile didn't fail to note the "extraordinary contrast" between the relatively free and spacious education in Toronto and "the old pedagogical notions" reigning in Catholic, traditional Montreal. [14]

A close associate of Coubertin in the 1890s was a man with very similar views with a very different social position. This was the orator, educator, and celebrated Dominican priest, Henri-Martin Didon (1840–1900). Like a few other restless Catholic leaders of his day, Père Didon interested himself in social problems, and he publicly expressed unorthodox views on divorce and the Trinity. These opinions, plus the sneering epithet "socialist" and news of the enormous crowds attending his sermons, brought him, in turn, fame, envy, accusations of arrogance, the attention of Rome, and temporary exile to Corsica. During his eighteen months' sojourn in Corsica, Didon wrote an essay on politics which he polished after six months of travel in Germany in 1882. *Les allemands* was published in Paris in 1884. It was the first popular French book to analyze dispassionately the reasons for Germany's successes. Didon's style was terse, but his message was portentous. He scolded France, and praised German discipline, patriotism, and devotion to public education. He noted the balance in German schools between intellectual and physical effort, which complemented each other. In his last years, Père Didon was the head of the Dominican lycée, Albert le Grand, in Paris. Coubertin called on him frequently at his residence on the rue St. Jacques, where they devised programs to introduce sports in Didon's school. (Some irate parents forced the conspirators to withdraw the program in boxing, which led Coubertin later to write that French parents were not yet "ripe" for this kind of activity.)[15] Didon, in return, lent his oratorical skills to the baron's ceremonial banquets and assemblies. It is worth noting here that chiseled in the stone over the entrance to Père Didon's school was the Latin motto, *Citius, Altius, Fortius* (Faster, Higher, Stronger).

For most of his life Coubertin's advocacy of physical education was only one aspect of his campaign for wholesale educational reform. Furthermore, his role as an educational theorist was only one part of a multi-faceted career that included high-level journalism and the writing of political history. Coubertin wrote articles in both American and French journals on the character and philosophy of various French politicans. Indeed, it is a tribute to the man's energy and stamina that his activities as a political reporter and historian reached their productive peak during the very years when he was most occupied with promoting international sporting festivals. In 1896 his *L'évolution française sous la troisième république* was published. In 1900 he began editing a newsletter, *Le Chronique de France*, on political and intellectual life, which appeared regularly until 1906. From 1902 until 1906 he regularly contributed "Pages d'histoire contemporaine" to the prestigious newspaper *Le Figaro*. Probably at Didon's urging, Coubertin also became a defender of a religious–social–political movement called the "Ralliément." The *ralliés* urged moderate social reform and proposed that the Church end its hostility to the (by then) established Third Republic.[16] Coubertin further condemned the nasty (and influential) journalism of Edouard Drumond, the author of *La France juive* (1886 and many later editions), as a spreader of *"le virus antisémite."*

From the great *cause célèbre* of French political and intellectual life at the fin de siècle, however, the Baron de Coubertin stayed almost entirely aloof. Rather late in the Dreyfus affair, Coubertin stated in an American magazine that he believed Alfred Dreyfus was guilty.[17] This was after the publication of Emile Zola's *J'accuse*, when it was myopic and perhaps vicious to make such a statement. One can suppose that, because of his liberal Catholicism and grudging republicanism on the one hand, and his loyalty to the aristocratic and military caste on the other, it would have destroyed him as a go-between to take some vigorous public position on the Dreyfus affair as almost every other person of his stature did.

After about 1908 the flow of Coubertin's journalism dwindled. He was already laboring over a large project which eventually appeared as his four-volume *Histoire universelle* in 1926 and 1927. The work is comparable to the grand conceptions of earlier, nineteenth-century historians, and those of Spengler and Toynbee, in its consideration of non-Western civilizations and its weighing of spiritual, economic, and demographic movements. Unfortunately, Coubertin's great history is the work of a disillusioned cynic and lacks the vitality and the occasional verbal *panache* of the man when he was younger. Other historians scarcely noticed his *Histoire universelle* and it was ignored by the public.

The successful institutionalization of the modern Olympic Games forced a rather specialized fame on Coubertin when he was aged. His ambitions had been grander, but he accepted this limited fame and even sought to intensify it in his last works in which he rehashed his earlier recorded adventures among the bureaucrats of patriotic and of cosmopolitan sport.

Coubertin published more than twenty books and hundreds of articles in his life.[18] His output demonstrates not only his vigor, but also indicates his influence in publishing circles as well as the fact that his fortune was large. Many of his publications were personally subsidized. He often complained that his burdens were heavy for his shoulders and for his purse. Almost the only writing which has endured is the small proportion which relates to the early years of Olympic movement. His many essays on education or physical education are interesting only in the French context, for they simply restate (or overstate) what was already well known abroad, particularly in the United States. As for his political journalism and historiography, though there are passages of wit and of memorable bitterness, most of his prose is dry and, perhaps worse, admonitory and didactic. [19] Only one of his early books, *L'évolution française sous la troisième république*, was translated. [20] Although he published several articles in American magazines such as the *Century*, editors had to prompt him to keep on the subject matter and off moralizing. [21] The modern reader must search to find the pithy statements that became increasingly infrequent as Coubertin got older. Unfortunately for the reputation Coubertin cultivated, his writing spanned those rich years when dazzling French stylists were not rare. The interested reader at the time had access to excellent writing on the same subjects (aside from athleticism, naturally) that were close to Coubertin's heart.

So many of Coubertin's projects came to nothing. His plans for the reform of all French education, together with his desires for a general revitalization of the whole French nation, were impossibly grandiose. He kept himself aloof from the back-biting, the bribery, and the opportunistic combinations of parliamentary politicians. He never attempted to influence the narrow bourgeois and provincials in the Chamber of Deputies. As he knew very well, the actual administration of France was in the hands of proud, highly trained, and deliberately insulated (from parliamentary or faddist pressure, that is) bureaucrats of the world's most centralized nation. The high-ranking French civil servants had their own esprit de corps and, of course, had a stake in defending the excellence of things as they were.

On the other hand, Baron Pierre de Coubertin had access to

Europe's titled aristocracy. He was close to many nonradical intellectuals. Besides Taine, Ernest Renan, and Jules Simon, whom he knew as old men, he was a friend of Père Didon, Pierre Barthelot, and Marshal Lyautey. He knew Jean Jaurès, Charles Maurras, and the great critic Eugène Melchior de Vogüé. All, incidentally, were better literary stylists than the prolific baron. An informal class solidarity required that Coubertin's claimed (and to some extent, acknowledged) aristocratic and literary peers lend at least their names to Coubertin's efforts to organize and channel sport.

Coubertin's projects and literary style obscure the real skills and many of the enduring contributions of the man who produced them. What makes a good administrator? Probably it is the stubborn determination to perform a possible task against conquerable odds. His efforts to influence effectively French civil servants may have amounted to little, but among the petty landlords, teachers in lycées, publishers, and the secretaries of local, warring athletic associations he was much more successful.[22] In his enthusiastic advocacy of sport, Coubertin was lucky. At the time, all kinds of athletic activities—amateur and professional, individual and organized—were booming in the Anglo-Saxon world. English sports (and even, to a small extent, gymnastics and turning) were growing in appeal in France without his efforts.[23] Since the Crystal Palace Exhibition of 1851, the new internationalism had been enriching and popularizing many activities that previously had been scattered and local. As Coubertin's sphere of operation became international he enlisted the help of American professors and Greek, Hungarian, and Swedish sporting officials and bureaucrats. Upon all of these he turned his fierce, unblinking eyes, his quick logic, and his astonishing energy—not to mention his perfection in costume, the cachet of the salons, and a noble name.

It is significant, and certainly ironic, that Coubertin rarely had contacts with athletes.[24] The people he prodded to action were bourgeois clubmen and skeptical foreign bureaucrats.

Audaciously and sagely, he employed techniques that would convince members of these groups. One technique was the banquet, with its soporific, hours-long program of toasts, speeches, wines, roasts, sauces, sweets, and oratorical tributes. He lulled his social and intellectual inferiors with affability that was not untinged with noblesse oblige and with his rhetoric, feasts, and music. He would present an assembly he had called with any of the great names he had been able to rally even briefly to the cause of physical education. Awed by his exaggeratedly optimistic programs and the aristocratic panache with which they were presented, indecisive club leaders were likely to subordinate any nascent projects they had had (an unlikely possibility) to those of the baron. He had the will the others lacked.

For the programs at his banquets and for his letterheads, Coubertin assembled lists of "honorary members" who had titles before their names, particles in the middle of their names, and lots of initials (indicating decorations and academic honors) after their names. His organization charts had grandeur: at the top of each was the name of a distinguished president, when possible a king, a prince, or the elected leader of a nation. But those who knew Coubertin well were aware that there was a direct, if invisible, line of authority that went directly to the "Secretary," Coubertin himself. He set up little offices with fine addresses and distributed free newsletters in large numbers. He wrote cheerful articles describing the progress of sport which he then planted in influential newpapers and reviews. With a haste that was suspect, he would arrange for his sporting organizations to have "anniversaries," solemn assemblies, and even an occasional "jubilee." Coubertin could invite dozens or hundreds of mildly curious (and gratefully freeloading) dignitaries to the "jubilee" of an organization that was little more than a list of names assembled at the top of an expensively printed letterhead that had been designed just a few years before.

Despite the logic of Coubertin's organizational concepts and

the size of his ambition, the impetus for his projects was heavily
dependent upon his personal fortune and his lonely will. He
had enthusiastically advocated for France a complex of activities that had grown quite naturally in English and American
society. Athletics were—and to some extent still remain—
rather antithetical to traditional French notions of "civilization." But one could not guess at Coubertin's many disappointments from reading the optimistic communiqués for publication
which came from his pen. His "Comité international olympique"—confidently referred to at the front of brochures, listed
at the top of letterheads, and accompanied by the five inter-
locking rings in the common colors representing those on all the
national flags—was for many years the frailest of paper structures. He was convinced that his portrayal of a French or
international sporting scene that was healthy and getting
healthier in 1894, 1904, and 1914 was justified, and surely
moral, though perhaps a little premature.

Coubertin's self-convincing enthusiasm led him into some
avant-garde, even eccentric, espousals of such things as nud-
ism—which activity, in those days of overdressing and cramped
modesty, he had to advocate as *bains d'air* ("air baths") and
eugenics. He also declared that it was manly for athletes to
bathe in water than had been scented with the "virile" perfumes: "I just cannot understand the pedants who pronounce a
sort of excommunication against perfumes in general and
against the so-called 'degenerates' who use them."[25] His
opinions on sports and peripheral matters were expressed in his
Revue olympique, a monthly he edited and published between
1901 and 1914. The journal served as the newsletter of the
Olympic movement as well as an outlet for his views. The most
intense espousal of athleticism to appear during these years was
his article in 1913, when Coubertin was fifty years old, entitled
"De la volupté sportive":

Yes, sport produces voluptuous sensations, that is to say, intense
physical pleasure. The man called upon to choose between the keen

pleasure that demeans him and the pleasure that exalts may well choose the second over the first. At the risk of showing a lack of respect for mythology, we suggest that it may not have been between vice and virtue that Hercules had to choose. This famous athlete very likely hesitated to choose between love and sport. And he pursued sport in the end.

Many sportsmen will swear that this pleasure reaches in certain circumstances the characteristics at once imperious and stirring of sexual passion. That these feelings are sensual is, in general, undeniable. It is infinitely probable that the animosity the early Christians unleashed against athleticism was due precisely to the fleshly satisfaction which sport represented as well as that "pride in life" pursued by sportsmen and denounced by the Holy Writ. [26]

Readers aware of certain fresh currents among Europe's intellectual elites during the decades when Coubertin was offering his philosophy may be tempted to trace the source of some of his views to another, more famous, personage. These glorifications of strenuous effort and devotion, and the speculation as to the great cultural innovations attributable to unleashed sensuality, bring to mind the intoxicating prose of Nietzsche. Though Coubertin never knew or praised the German philosopher, it occasionally seems that they breathed the same air. Coubertin, when young, was despondent about French overrefinement and later he extended his criticism to the whole modern world, which he was convinced was becoming too diverse, too torpid, and decadent. The German philosopher and the French administrator were both elitists, convinced that the world should be commanded by a species of self-elevated superman, single-minded enough to disregard the prevailing and debilitating standards of comfort (as opposed to pleasure, which *was* to be sought). Both loathed artistic mediocrity. Coubertin shared the German's exalted pleasure in music and always hoped to elevate musical competitions to the level of sporting competitions in international festivals. Both praised action as an abstract principle and as a tonic to raise actual and potential elites from the morass of ease and possessions that both felt were destroying culture. Naturally, after the calamities brought about by the mindless use of force in two world wars, the reputations of both men have suffered. One critic of certain tendencies in modern sport has said of Pierre de Coubertin that "as a political thinker, he must be considered a forerunner of totalitarianism."[27]

Like the social Darwinists who were gathering adherents and vociferousness in European intellectual circles at the same time, Coubertin claimed that aggression was spontaneous and ineradicable in human nature and suggested that sport could divert and dilute destructive passions on the playing fields and thus help us to sidestep much human wreckage. Even if war was inevitable, "an army of sportsmen would be more human, more pitying in the struggle and more calm and gentle afterward. There is no good reason to doubt this." Sport, "the abstraction of physical effort," showed exceptional individuals the way to physical euphoria. Competition of an intense though non-destructive kind among the world's elites would lead to a consequent expansion of the human spirit and give rise, among the best humans, to a more delicate sense of justice, a broadening of views, and a more constructive employment of energy.

Though Coubertin customarily presented his views with optimistic rhetoric, as a political and educational reformer he was hardly democratic or cheerful about human nature. In the early years of the modern Olympic movement, for example, he opposed the construction of huge stadiums for the masses, believing that the mindless agitation of ignorant onlookers would only distract the best athletes. He felt that the supreme athlete, or, more correctly, the superior person who submitted himself to "a virile education," exalted himself to a condition that was its own reward. The masses of men were selfish and at once lazy and potentially violent and disruptive. From the beginning his educational schemes were intended to keep most of the people distracted, busy, and useful. He wished to see France make the most of her economic and human resources.

His late projects for "workers' universities" had behind them the desire, not necessarily democratic, to make the most efficient use of the national resources of energy and intelligence. Coubertin's most original perception, and one which he developed into an aesthetic that has become deeply ingrained in the modern Olympic movement, is the notion that sport must be presented as theater.[28] If the reader of Coubertin's prose is puzzled by the lack of references to actual sporting activities or to particular athletes, he is also likely to be struck by the obvious relish and expansiveness with which Coubertin describes the festivals, the ceremonies, the rituals that he devised to promote his causes. A "congress," a "jubilee," or any meeting of athletes had to have a setting, a theme, continuity, intermissions, and a suitably prepared audience.

English sport, which he at first wished to use to toughen Frenchmen, was not, Coubertin feared, a readily transferable taste. His intended public—at first Frenchmen, later the world—had to be "seduced" (he used this word in this context) and charmed into participating in or supporting athletic competition. Meets had to have superstructures of dramatic sequence and settings of natural or architectural beauty.[29] Accordingly, in Paris in the early 1890s, Coubertin's first rowing meets, gymnastic competitions, and "cross-countrys" (the English term had to be used) were preceded by banquets; interspersed with parades, speeches, and presentations of awards; and finished off with solemn assemblies which often took place at night and were accompanied with fireworks displays or torchlit processions.

Coubertin wanted his Olympic festivals to carry gracefully the opening ceremonies, the ranking of dignitaries, pretentious slogans, banners, medals stamped with allegories, and all the pseudoclassical trappings that had already come into use in the international expositions. It was his view that sport must be theater and conceivably even "cult" or "religion," (he also used these words). All this Coubertin succeeded in implanting among the cosmopolitan bureaucrats of international Olympism.

Another enduring, if dubious, contribution of Coubertin was the tenet that might be called "the Olympic paradox." This is the contradictory notion, stated repeatedly by Coubertin and maintained by the priests of modern Olympism ever since, that international sporting competition both intensifies patriotism and prevents political friction owing to opposed nationalistic ambitions—that, in other words, the mixing of patriotism and competition will somehow further universal peace. In an article written just after the Athens Games of 1896, Coubertin stated:

One may be filled with a desire to see the color of one's club or college triumph in a national meeting; but how much stronger is the feeling when the colors of one's country are at stake! I am well assured that the victors in the Stadion at Athens wished for no other recompense when they heard the people cheer the flag of their country in honor of their achievement.

It was with these thoughts in mind that I sought to revive the Olympic Games. I have succeeded after many efforts. Should this institution prosper—as I am persuaded, all civilized nations aiding, that it will—it may be a potent, if indirect, factor in securing universal peace. Wars break out because nations misunderstand each other. We shall not have peace until the prejudices which now separate the different races shall have been outlived. To attain this end, what better means than to bring the youth of all countries periodically together for amicable trials of muscular strength and agility? The Olympic Games, with the ancients, controlled athletics and promoted peace. Is it not visionary to look to them for similar benefactions in the future?[30]

Among the many enduring disappointments of Pierre de Coubertin was the casualness with which his devotions were accepted by the decision-making elites of the Third Republic. Ministers of education and subministers merely thanked him for his laboriously assembled projects for educational transformation. The Frenchmen of Coubertin's time remained far behind the Americans, the Hungarians, the Finns, and (grim irony!) the Germans in their adoption of Anglo-Saxon sport.

The French did not give Coubertin *consideration* or the honor that he felt he merited. This will be clearly seen in the discussions of his efforts to stage proper, modern Olympic Games in Paris in 1900. On the other hand, Coubertin's depiction of himself as a universal genius and an organizational wizard found ever greater acceptance abroad. His reputation, however, was based on the popularity and usefulness of the Olympic Games, and not upon the projects that inspired the great bulk of his writing—particularly in his early years.

The process by which Coubertin acquired fame took a while. After the disappointments of 1900, the former patriot and *revanchard* became more tolerant and cosmopolitan. He eventually consented to the awarding of the sixth modern Olympic Games (scheduled for 1916) to Berlin. When he emigrated to Switzerland in 1918, he left behind a France more blasé than ungrateful. In Lausanne, projects for new educational systems, essays on colonialism, and more books poured from his pen, but the admiring world remained interested only in his ever more abstract observations on modern international sport.

4

ORGANIZATION

*P*IERRE DE COUBERTIN had the historian's sensitivity and need for periodization. In his memoirs he stressed the importance of particular dates and turning points—the historian's punctuation. He dated the campaign for the revival of the Olympic Games from an article he published in *Le français* on August 30, 1887. Shortly before, he had returned from one of his henceforth-to-be frequent trips to England. There had been a running debate in the French bourgeois magazines over the excessive demands made on pupils in the schools. Coubertin in his article proposed that French children be required to do yet more, that they be introduced to sports and games. He proposed that new schools have playgrounds, that there be regular physical instruction, and that leagues be established to promote sporting competitions between the lycées. The benefit to the public, he claimed, would be increased alertness and a better use of the pupils' intelligence. The children would understand better and learn twice as fast.

Some readers attacked Coubertin's "vulgar" proposition. Since the author referred respectfully to English education, he was attacked as a bad Frenchman.[1] Coubertin was satisfied with the attention, some of it sympathetic, that he attracted by his proposals. He proceeded thereafter to make more inclusive the projected scope of his League for Physical Education, the formation of which he also announced in the article in *Le français*.

Coubertin wished to gather the reins of control of French amateur and educational sport, such as they were, into his own hands. Accordingly, he called on the officials of various sporting bodies and requested them to join him. His journalistic work increased. He later claimed that a scrapbook for the period May 15–August 15, 1887, contained seventy-one articles about his speeches and other promotional activities for sport in Paris.[2] He did not hesitate to use his distinguished name to gain access to important French politicians, most of whom were then preoccupied with preparations for the Universal Exposition of 1889 in Paris. Indicative of his success were the ministerial decrees between November, 1888, and March, 1889, which provided for a "Congress for Physical Education" which was to take place in June, 1889. A curious characteristic of this "Congress" was that the entire responsibility for organizing and financing it fell to Coubertin. Time was short. Coubertin could ferret out no royalty to come to his congress, but he did capture Jules Simon, a republican politician and bureaucrat. Simon was famous for his patriotic oratory, which could bring many Frenchmen to tears.

Though ministerially empowered to charge five francs admission to his meetings, Coubertin distributed six hundred free tickets to pupils of the lycées, their families, and some journalists for the sporting events scheduled for the first two weeks in June. An exhibition of horse riding had divisions for juniors (under fifteen years) and for seniors, and attracted 150 participants. The fencing competition took place in the great hall of the Grand Hotel, to which Coubertin attracted many members of aristocratic families. For background music he obtained the Rumanian band which happened to be in Paris for the exposition. Coubertin was embarrassed when his program of June 10 for fifteen track and field events (called *sports athlétiques* after the English use of "athletics") attracted few spectators from the lycées and colleges. There were, however, three hundred entries, and the events were held as scheduled, as was a "rallaye" (cross-country race) the next day in a forest near Paris. Coubertin also recruited some competitors for swimming competitions. He arranged for a parade of horses, a demonstration of football (soccer), a rowing exhibition, a demonstration of tennis, and a procession down the Seine of "huit yoles à quatre et un outrigger à deux de pointe."[3]

The formal opening of the congress proper was on June 15, 1889, in the Ecole des ponts et chausées. Those few in attendance were stirred by Jules Simon's speech calling on them to celebrate at this congress the return to French gaity, to the old Gallic gaity and to the valor of the body which is the companion of a gallant spirit."[4] There were also business meetings, lunches, buffets, punches, and, as accompaniment to these many social occasions, music and speeches. Coubertin publicly attributed the organizing of this congress to a "Comité Jules Simon," which was named after its president. Pierre de Coubertin, needless to add, was secretary. The congress closed with a ceremony in the great amphitheater of the Sorbonne. Coubertin presented awards, similar to those given in the artistic and industrial competitions of the great exposition, to winners in the sporting competitions. The astonished Simon slipped him a note saying, "What's this? You awarding the medals? Well, I suppose we owe you this, since you have yourself made up the whole show."

Long afterward Coubertin confessed that his "League" and his "Committee" were "monumental façades" and that his actions were made possible through his influence and publicity.[5] His success in acquiring prominence annoyed the patriots in some of the little sports clubs and some members of the exclusive clubs of the rich. Coubertin's critics felt that his particular kinds of organized muscularity were symptoms of a British disease and that the little Anglophile was its carrier. One nationalist claimed that the baron wished to "import into France British interschool sports just as one imports hunting dogs and racehorses."[6] And he was attacked as the author of

deplorable festivities which are becoming much too frequent, especially at examination time. These repeated competitions threaten to
throw studies into disarray and actually to bring about the pupils'
physical exhaustion. These inconveniences have, incidentally, been
accompanied by an exaggerated amount of noisy and outrageous
publicity. [7]

Coubertin had intended from the beginning that his staged festivals would be reported favorably and, if necessary, otherwise in
the press. Henceforth he was a much discussed sports bureaucrat.

Just after the congress of 1889 ended Coubertin called on the
president of the Republic, Sadi Carnot, who appointed him an
"official" representative of France for Coubertin's first visit to
America. He sailed from Le Havre in September, 1889. On the
way back he stopped in England, where he began his friendship
with Dr. W. P. Brookes. Coubertin was an enchanted spectator
at Brookes's "Olympic Games" in Much Wenlock. [8] Upon his
return to France Coubertin was more convinced than ever about
the usefulness of Anglo-Saxon sport. He had assured himself of
the benefits of the "régime arnoldien," a term he applied to the
common practice in English and American education of inte-
grating physical education into public instruction. In France he
was gaining public notoriety along with some cautious official
support. He started regular publication of the *Revue athlétique*,
which grew to sixty-four pages a month, and he continued his
campaign to unify organized sport.

Although French sport was retarded when compared with
developments in Scandinavia, Germany, and Great Britain,
various kinds of new recreational activities were making head-
way in France in the 1880s and 1890s. [9] In addition to the
ancient French recreations of fencing and riding, there were
such new ones as rowing, cycling, track competitions, swimming,
and others. In Paris there were even a few groups of gymnasts
and turners. Although many of these activities were rather new
in France, and their practitioners were mostly confined to the

area around Paris, they had clubs known by their initials, occasional newsletters, and leaders who, like Coubertin, were often ideologically inspired. The clubs had memberships drawn from different classes. The cyclists, for example, who were likely to be lower bourgeois or working class craftsmen, were very different from the rowers who were likely to be wealthy or aristocratic. The clubs had different views of patriotism and subtly different, but usually irreconcilable, views of the respective roles of amateurs and professionals in sport. These years were also those in which the French sporting press was founded. This small but diversified and dynamic sporting scene was Coubertin's field of operation.

It serves little purpose to go into all or even many of the mergers, splits, name changes, recruiting drives, and meetings that Coubertin arranged in the two decades after 1887. Most of these maneuvers occupied much space in Coubertin's consciousness and in his memoirs, but had little impact either on French sport or on the Olympic movement. In any case, after his return from America late in 1889, Coubertin once again began to gather together the French sporting clubs. He got a group of cyclists to join him, though he did not especially like the sport. Nor did he care for several other sports that joined his Union des sociétés françaises des sports athlétiques (henceforth U.S.F.S.A.). He was, however, especially eager to take over boxing:

I thought it beneficial to practice the many sports (*braves récréations*) in the lycées and an excellent auxiliary to promote the rapid virilisation of our youth. [10]

Coubertin had a rival in another federation called the Ligue de l'éducation physique, which was rather well financed because it included polo, ballooning, and sailing—all activities of the prosperous. He was under pressure to join the Ligue under its organizers' terms, and Coubertin's "President," Jules Simon, even threatened to resign if Coubertin remained aloof. But in

1891 ballooning and sailing joined the U.S.F.S.A., and the Ligue began disintegrating. Coubertin merged his *Revue athlétique* with the Ligue's *Sports athlétiques.* Someone donated a suite of offices with a few chairs and a green carpet. At the second "general assembly" of the U.S.F.S.A. on July 5, 1891, Coubertin claimed in his speech thirty-two affiliates representing two thousand active members and—he was proud of this— 120 honorary members. In a speech he announced: "French athleticism *exists.* It is still in its infancy, I know full well. But it exists and, since it exists and it is French, I know it will triumph!"[11]

His meetings and his sports events had festive auxiliaries. A "cross-country" race in the Bois de Boulogne was followed by a "lunch" (for both the event and the repast English words were used). Despite "Siberian" temperatures at a football game, he attracted as spectators Lord and Lady Dufferin. After the game there was a "punch" at the Restaurant de Madrid. He also arranged for a demonstration by an American rowing team and, working through the American ambassador, he arranged for a son and a daughter of President Harrison to be present as spectators.

An enduring concern of Coubertin was with obtaining a proper, open football field in the Bois de Boulogne. He noted that one existing field had a "homicidal" tree in its center: "Oh but it was miserable, ugly and stunted. One played around it. The players were constantly in danger of a collision." Finally the elderly director of public works in Paris decreed the death of the tree, but the man died before the tree did.[12]

During these years Coubertin also made tours in the provinces to gather more affiliates for the U.S.F.S.A. Though his organization was small and had changed names three times in its short history, Coubertin confidently planned a "jubilee" of the Union des sociétés françaises des sports athlétiques for November 27, 1892. Although he wasn't on hand for the celebration, the president of the Republic, Sadi Carnot, was "patron." Grand Duke Vladimir of Russia actually appeared. Another catch was Jean Jules Jusserand, a French diplomat who had served in Britain and who, like Coubertin, hoped for a regeneration of French sport.[13] Sports demonstrations by French lycée and university students preceded the meetings. There was a bicycle race before the inaugural breakfast and a fencing competition before the official ceremony opening a new clubhouse. The astronomer Pierre Janssen gave a copious lunch after a cross-country race. At the frequent banquets Coubertin read congratulatory telegrams from the provinces.

The meetings upon which Coubertin placed the greatest importance for the jubilee of 1892 were the closing sessions, for which he had obtained the grand amphitheater of the Sorbonne. The old hall was festooned with neoclassical ornaments and lined with the sculpted busts of the giants of French literature. These meetings were not much concerned with organizational matters, as they had been taken care of beforehand. For the occasion, a musician friend of Coubertin composed music for a Sophoclean ode which a soprano sang for the guests. Among the many attractions was a little comedy in verse by "Paul de Frédy" (a pseudonym of Pierre's brother). The title of the piece was "Dante et Virgil à l'union des sports."[14]

The intellectual meat of the assembly was a three-part historical discussion of sport. One Georges Bourdon spoke of sport in the lives of the classical Greeks and read some translations of Pindar. Jusserand spoke on sport in medieval and Renaissance France. He quoted texts of Villon, Rabelais, and Montaigne which exalted competitive games and praised the trained, healthy body. Coubertin spoke on "Physical Exercises in the Modern World." He cited statistics demonstrating the particularly rapid growth abroad in athletic participation and competition. As usual, he drew his figures from a questionnaire on "le régime arnoldien" which he had sent out years before.

Coubertin had intended that the last paragraphs of his speech would have the greatest impact:

There are people who talk about the elimination of war; those who treat these people as utopians are not wrong. But there are others who talk about the progressive diminution of the chances of war and I don't see that as utopian at all. It is clear that the telegraph, railroads, the telephone, dedicated research congresses and expositions have done more for peace than all the treaties and diplomtic conventions. Indeed, I expect that athleticism will do even more.

Those who have seen 30,000 people tramp through the rain to watch a football match will know that I am not exaggerating. Let us export our rowers, our runners, and our fencers: that will be the free trade of the future. When the day comes that this is introduced into the customs of old Europe, the progress toward peace will receive a powerful, new impulse. . . .

All this leads to what we should consider the second part of our program. I hope you will help us in the future as you have in the past to pursue this new project. What I mean is that, on a basis conforming to modern life, we reestablish a great and magnificent institution, the Olympic Games.

That was it! This was Coubertin's first public proposal for the ultimate step in the internationalization of sport. [15] Coubertin's excitement as he uttered these last words was not shared by the audience of lycée pupils, teachers, club officials, intellectuals, friends, and a few adversaries. Some were puzzled; he might just as well have suggested a resurrection of the Eleusinian mysteries or the oracle at Delphi. For others it was an occasion for inventive fantasy. Could he possibly mean a restoration of a cult celebration valid more than two thousand years ago? Could we require modern athletes to participate in the radically simple costume the judges demanded of competitors in ancient times? Would our Olympic Games be solely for Frenchmen or could we include a few foreigners? Redskins from America? Heathen Chinese? Negroes?

Coubertin's notions of what form the projected international games would take were, in any case, vague. He did, nonetheless, begin at once to plan for an international meeting of sports bureaucrats who could also consider the matter. In the meantime, Coubertin continued to promote sport in specific ways. A near miracle had occurred in October, 1892, when an invited team of English rowers was defeated by a French team in a race at Andresy on the Seine. Immediately after the jubilee of 1892, Coubertin began preparing for the entry of a French team of rowers at the regatta at Henley the following summer. Unfortunately, however, the loose confederation of the U.S.F.S.A. contained three separate rowing societies, each of them feuding with the others. Who would be on the team? Who would pay their expenses? What expenses? There followed confrontations of irreconcilable, standard distances and public correspondence in the societies' newsletters claiming treachery. The hottest debates were over the definition of "amateur." Two societies allowed money prizes. Coubertin overcame all objections by choosing a composite team and by persuading all the French to accept the British rules. But rowing in Great Britain was a sport belonging to a much higher social class than in France. Would the British accept the whole French team? Not only did the Amateur Rowing Association forbid awards of money, but any person who did manual labor was barred from their competitions. Eventually the English agreed to ignore the demeaning occupations of a couple of members of the French team.

The locomotive that pulled the French team into Henley in the summer of 1893 was draped with a French tricolor and was greeted by cheers. Coubertin himself was one of the judges along the course. For a while during the race, as in Paris, the French team was leading. A boat from the Thames Rowing Club, however, bumped it and deflected the French into a barrier whereupon the Thames rowers dashed ahead to win. Coubertin refused to claim a foul, fearing that he might jeopardize future Anglo-French cooperation and competition. Then succumbing to pressure from the French fans around him, he lodged a complaint, only to withdraw it shortly afterwards. Later the English newspapers praised the French for being noble losers, but the "crise de rowing" stayed with Coubertin for years afterward in Paris.[16] All the same he went ahead with preparation for a meet between the Association vélocepidique d'amateurs and the (English) National Cyclists' Union as well as a match between some amateur French and English footballers.

In the fall if 1893 Coubertin was an official representative of the Third Republic at the World's Columbian Exposition in Chicago. This world's fair was to celebrate the four hundredth anniversary of the discovery of the hemisphere, but it opened a year late. The great fair in Chicago was America's most ambitious attempt to rival the French international expositions. Coubertin's main object in being there was to attend an international congress on higher education, and he also traveled extensively around the country. He spoke at Tulane University and established prizes for public speaking at the University of California in Berkeley and at Princeton. Much of the three weeks he was at Princeton he spent with Professor William Milligan Sloane, of whom it has been written:

Powerful in build, hearty in manner, genial, urbane, Sloane resembled the diplomat and man of affairs rather than the typical professor. . . . Fluent in conversation, abounding in pithy anecdote and witty allusion, possessed of an extraordinary knowledge of unusual things, he moved always in a circle of friendship and appreciation.[17]

Both men were historians. At the time, Sloane was nearing the end of his four-volume biography of Napoleon.[18] We have no reliable record of their conversations, but it seems likely that Coubertin's views as to what forms the new Olympic Games might take acquired a little precision at this time.

The ambiance at Princeton probably inspired Coubertin. The campus in the autumn of 1893 was, of course, lovely and looked as respectable as that of the English universities which Coubertin admired and after which Princeton was modeled. The "sports craze" was underway there and Sloane supported it. Sloane even arranged for Coubertin to present his ideas on

international sports meets to some men at the University Club in
New York. They predicted his failure.[19] On his way back to
Paris in December, 1893, Coubertin also spent several days in
London. There he met Mr. C. Herbert, the secretary of the
Amateur Athletic Association. Herbert was eager to devise an
internationally acceptable definition of "amateur" that would
permit English teams to travel yet farther than they had been
doing. But later, at a dinner at the Sports Club in London,
Coubertin could rouse no interest in the Olympic Games.

When Coubertin returned to Paris, he found the city and
indeed his contacts in the government well immersed in
preparations for the greatest world's fair of all time, the one
scheduled for Paris in 1900. The first decrees preparing for this
exposition had been published very early, in July, 1892, to
forestall rumored preparations of the Germans to present a great
world's fair in Berlin in 1900. Like almost all Frenchman,
Coubertin was eager to assist in assuring the triumph of this
grandiose manifestation of French cultural superiority. He had
managed to include his modest meeting on physical education
within the embrace of the Exposition of 1889. The Exposition of
1900 was to be grander in every way. For one thing, it was to be
emphatically more international. Thus Coubertin was willing,
even eager, to include a much more ambitious sports congress
in the next exposition.

He had seen to it that at a meeting of the U.S.F.S.A. in the
spring of 1893 that he, as the organization's secretary, would be
authorized to issue invitations for an "International Athletic
Congress." Accordingly, upon his return to Paris from America
and Britain, Coubertin designed a circular announcing that a
congress was to be held from June 16 to June 24, 1894.[20] The
circular contained a list of officers for the congress that
included Professor Sloane, Mr. Herbert of London, Captain
Viktor Balck, a sports enthusiast from Sweden, and one
F. Kemeny, director of a school in Hungary. Most of the ten-
point program set forth for discussion the various problems of

amateurism. Some sample questions: Could one be a professional in one sport and an amateur in another? If art objects are to be given as prizes, how can we limit their value? If admission is charged, should the money go to the clubs or to the competitors? Is betting consistent with amateurism? The last three points for discussion in the suggested program appeared under the subtitle, "Olympic Games." The three points to be discussed were the possibility of reestablishing the Games, what sort of sports to include, and the establishment of an international committee. Coubertin adopted as the slogan for the congress the motto, *Citius, Fortius, Altius.*

In January, 1894, Coubertin sent the circular to all the athletic clubs abroad for which he addresses. He was reasonably assured of respectable attention within France, but he quickly became aware that his international connections were lopsidedly Anglo-Saxon. No one in Holland or Switzerland answered his circular, and he knew nobody in Germany. There were, of course, good reasons why he should know nobody in Germany. He was above all a French patriot. As a sport organizer he knew that the largest and best-organized sports clubs in the world were those of the turners, whose philosophy of physical education was the very opposite of that of the English, which was cosmopolitan and elitist and which he favored. Nonetheless, Coubertin called at the German embassy in Paris where he met with the military attaché, Colonel Max von Schwartzkoppen, to obtain the names of German sports officials. [21] He did this little more than a month before the congress was to open. Before any German could respond, however, the leader of the Union des sociétés gymnastiques declared that if the Germans were invited the French gymnasts would withdraw. Eventually a German living in London, Baron von Rieffenstein, appeared at the congress, but he was declared "unofficial" so that several French patriots could participate and still save face.

The continental gymnasts and turners—Swedish, Belgian,

French, or German—always were troublesome for Coubertin. It was not only their touchy patriotism and blatant paramilitarism, it was also their dogmatism and the anti-individualism of their ideology. Basic to the position of all gymnasts was that sport was one thing and gymnastics was quite another. But there were many kinds of mutually exclusive gymnastics (including German turning) in the 1890s. Before and after Coubertin's Paris congress of 1894 the Belgian gymnasts sent vituperative propaganda all over Europe denouncing what little they knew of Coubertin's plans.

Somehow, on Saturday, June 16, 1894, at 4:15 in the afternoon, Coubertin managed to fill the grand amphitheater of the new Sorbonne with two thousand people. They were academicians, politicians, bureaucrats, and students. The hall was decorated with a fresco of classical themes by Puvis de Chavannes called "The Sacred Grove." One of Coubertin's heroes, President Sadi Carnot, had been inaugurated there, and the hall was used for such ceremonies as the jubilee marking Louis Pasteur's birth. Thereafter, in the periodization that the historian Pierre de Coubertin established for the Olympic movement, the eight-day meeting was usually memorialized as "The Congress of the Sorbonne."

Representatives from Italy, Spain, Russia, and even Greece appeared at the congress. There were, in all, seventy-nine delegates from forty-nine societies in twelve countries. Coubertin later confessed that in the course of his meeting he had planned "to please and impress" the delegates and that he wished "not to convince, but to seduce."[22] Accordingly, he planned unusually elaborate fêtes and was more than usually meticulous in creating an atmosphere that would lead the delegates to believe that they themselves were making history. Boldly Coubertin had inscribed on the invitations to the opening session, "Congress for the Reestablishment of the Olympic Games."

Baron de Courcel, the French ambassador to Berlin, opened

the proceedings with a short, formal speech. The poet Jean Aicard's talk, which was supposed to be on "La force et le droit," celebrated athleticism. More inspring addresses followed. Then came the pièce de résistance.

There had been an extraordinary and happy discovery in Athens a year before. The French school there unearthed some previously unknown antique poems on marble tablets. The words had mysterious signs over them which turned out to be musical notation. The signs over a "Hymn to Apollo," which was two-thirds intact, were deciphered. This music was the longest extant example of an element of life in ancient Hellas that was as essential as their athleticism, about which almost infinitely more was known. The illustrious French composer, Gabriel Fauré, then composed a choral accompaniment to the rediscovered music. When performed, this noble relic was, oddly enough, much closer to Richard Wagner's radical compositions than to the sharp contrapuntalism of traditional European art music. Early in 1894 Faure's orchestration of the Greek music had been performed in Athens, Constantinople, Brussels, and Paris. The music was exciting, evoking splendors once thought irrevocably past. [23] It was a voice from the tomb. Thus when Madame Jeanne Remacle, supported by harps and the chorus, sang the "Hymn to Apollo" at Coubertin's congress, the delegates and other participants felt inspired by Hellenism, its idealism and history. According to Coubertin, a mood reigned that one "expected only in sacred services."[24]

After this noble and joyous beginning, the fêtes continued for the delegates, especially the foreign delegates. Coubertin had them invited to lunches at the Paris town houses of men who had titles. There was a reception at the Ministry of the Interior. The Racing Club of Paris gave a "Fête de nuit." There were foot races of 150, 500, and 3,000 meters on June 21. The lawn of the Crois catelan was surrounded with a thousand torches as the delegates watched a military parade in which there were more torches. This display was followed by trumpet voluntaries,

military music, and fireworks. Throughout the stay of the delegates there were more parades with lanterns, banners, and
music. The delegates saw races and exhibitions for yachts and
for bicycles. At the lunch at the tennis club the table decorations were miniatures of all the national flags in the world.
Almost all the delegates gave speeches on one occasion or
another.

Early in the proceedings the congress divided into two
committees. French sports organizers discussed amateurism. In
general, Coubertin's views prevailed. He always opposed the
tendency of the ignorant public to turn superior athletes into
circus performers. In their correspondence Sloane and Coubertin customarily referred to amateur sport as "clean" sport. Yet,
on the other hand, the delegates condemned those British
sporting clubs that excluded working men from their competitions. If an athlete were to be compensated at all, there were
attempts to distinguish between money as a reward for performance and as an indemnity for time lost from work while
training and performing.

The other commission, on Olympism, was nominally headed
by Demitrios Bikelas (1835–1908), the delegate from Athens.
He was, like Coubertin and Sloane, a historian, and he had also
written novels. His works on Byzantium and on Greece in
medieval times were known in English and French translations.
Bikelas had also translated some of Shakespeare into modern
Greek and had written some Greek patriotic songs. Sloane was
the vice-president of the committee on Olympism. The other
foreign delegates proceeded in accordance with the principles
the organizer had made known in advance. Indeed, Coubertin
had published an article, "Le rétablissement des jeux olympiques," in the *Revue de Paris* on June 15, 1894—that is, at the
same time that the congress was meeting.[25] In the article, as at
the congress, Coubertin stated principles and did not invite
much discussion of them. Some of the specific recommen-
dations that the committee agreed on were these:

1. Like the ancient festivals, the modern Olympic Games should take place every four years.
2. The revived Olympics (unlike the ancient Games) would be modern and international. The sports would be those of the nineteenth century.
3. The Games would be for adults (only Bikelas and Balck had pressed for contests for children).
4. Strict definitions of "amateur" would apply. Money would be used only for organization, facilities, and festivities.
5. The modern Olympic Games must be, to use Coubertin's expression, "ambulatory." Coubertin claimed that the festivals would be too expensive for any one nation to offer repeatedly.

A most important part of the work of the Bikelas committee was to establish the International Olympic Committee, the members of which were to represent the principles of modern Olympism to their home countries. Sloane, Balck, and Bikelas were, of course, to be members. To fill the roster of members of the first I.O.C., Coubertin provided a list of names. He would inform several of the other members of their elevation to this distinction by mail. Their presence in Paris or even their interest in the committee was not a necessary prerequisite for eligibility. In short, the secretary, Pierre de Coubertin, was the whole "International Olympic Committee."

The congress continued to go along smoothly. Jovial and expansive Professor Sloane moved among all the delegates keeping his and Coubertin's views of Olympism before them. Balck was enthusiastic and proposed Stockholm as a site for the first modern Games. For some time Coubertin had rather expected and had led everyone to believe that the first Olympic Games of the modern era would take place in Paris in 1900 as part of the Universal Exposition.

A curious, bogus Hellenic intrusion into the flow of the program was the suggestion of Professor Michel Bréal (1832–1915), a friend of Coubertin and a distinguished classical philologist. He offered a silver cup as a trophy for a "Marathon race" which he proposed as an event for the first modern Olympic Games. He named the race after the Athenian victory at Marathon, after which, according to the legend embroidered over the centuries, a certain Pheidippides ran forty kilometers and expired after announcing, "Rejoice, we have won." Coubertin thanked Bréal for his proposal and returned to important matters.

The little baron seems himself to have been transported into a euphoric state by the atmosphere he created. The final dinner was held in the Jardin d'acclimatisation on June 23, 1894. None of the other speeches by Sloane, Bikelas, or other have survived, but Coubertin's closing words reveal his extreme satisfaction and a great deal of his style. Characteristically, he saw enemies (the old school) and friends (the press) where there were none, and he was aggressively optimistic as well as traditionally, if clumsily, rhetorical:

We have been brought together in Paris, this grand metropolis, whose joys and anxieties are shared by the whole world to such an extent that one can say that we meet at the nerve center of the world. We are the representatives of international athletics and we voted unanimously (for it appears that the principle is scarcely controversial at all) for the restoration of an idea that is two thousand years old. But this idea still quickens the hearts of men in whom it stimulates the instincts . . . that are the most noble and the most vital. In a great temple of science, our delegates have heard the modern echo of a melody which is also two thousand years old and was resurrected by a scholarly archaeologist who based his work upon that of preceding generations. And this evening electricity transmitted everywhere the news that the Olympism of ancient Hellas has reemerged in the world after an eclipse of many centuries. . . .

Some of the adherents of the old school wailed that we held our meeting openly in the heart of the Sorbonne. They knew full well that we are rebels and that we would climax our proceedings by bringing down the structure of their worm-eaten philosophy. That is true, gentlemen! We are rebels and that is why the members of the press, who have always supported beneficial revolutions, have understood us and helped us, for which, by the way, I thank them with all my heart.

I astonish myself and apologize, gentlemen, for having employed rhetoric like this and for having taken you to such lofty heights. If I were to continue, the champagne might evaporate, leaving boredom. Therefore I hasten to propose a toast again. I raise my glass to the Olympic idea which, like a ray of the all–powerful sun, has pierced the mists of the ages to illuminate the threshold of the twentieth century with joy and hope.[26]

Though his mood was not (as claimed) shared by the world at large, it certainly was shared by the other delegates. The conference had proceeded triumphantly. Might the delegates be risking the dissipation of euphoria in the six years that remained until the Universal Exposition in Paris? What about having the first Olympic Games four years earlier, in 1896? Balck already had authorization to offer Stockholm as the site. Or, on the other hand, might the delegates not consider the more sunny climate and the more redolent air of Greece itself? Shortly after the opening of the last session of the congress, Coubertin whispered something into Bikelas's ear. Bikelas nodded. The proposal was made public. All those on hand murmured for a while and then the motion was carried unanimously.[27] Athens would be the site of the first revived Olympic Games, just two years hence. The king of Greece had already sent Coubertin a telegram dated June 21, 1894, thanking the members of the congress for "the reestablishment of the Olympic Games."

Coubertin's "Congress of the Sorbonne" was designed to attract publicity. His own article assuring the public that the new Olympic Games would be modern appeared in the bourgeois–intellectual *Revue de Paris*. There were respectful notices in a few of the French newspapers, but nothing like a wave of interest either for or against. Reaction in the press abroad was not heartening, since it was scattered and weak. One English observer, as he brooded over the attempt to reinstitute the

Olympics asked the question, "Could this flower bloom but once?" Recalling the "harmonious ensemble" of classical athletes, he went on:

The only classes in the modern world whose interest in athletics is wholly genuine and unfeigned are professionals, idle young amateurs of wealth, a few educators, and the least studious among our college youths. The rest of the world is ready to be amused by their performances and loudly vociferates its approval of the gospel of physical culture, but the real leaders of life and thought can never again contemplate an athletic contest with the emotions of men who, like the poets, philosophers and statesmen of Greece, spent the best days of their youth in the gymnasium and often made it the centre of their social and intellectual life in maturer years. [28]

Another writer was irritated at the high tone of Coubertin's pronouncements and noted that "athletic youths are no more amiable than average youths and the nations that read of their feats are just as likely to grow spiteful as amiable over them." The discussions of international athletic events, he said, are unlikely to be "marked by any politeness or excess of literary suavity" and, furthermore,

as none of the contestants will be naked and nobody will be killed or seriously injured, and as those who drive will ride in chariots with springs, and those who race horses will ride in saddles, the resemblance to the ancient games will not be very close, but still, beyond a certain waste of money, there will be no harm in the new whim. [29]

Paradoxically, it was in Germany that Coubertin's projects got the most attention, but the bulk of the publicity was precipitated almost accidentally and came very late. Shortly after the Sorbonne congress, news of the projected, French-sponsored Olympic Games was the occasion for editorial writers in several turning newsletters to reiterate yet again their opposition to elitist, high-performance, spectator-oriented, Anglo-Saxon sport. If the Germans were to participate in modern Olympic Games, they would have to be *national* Olympic Games for

Germans alone.[30] On the other hand, there was a growing sport movement in Germany that made its way in spite of the turners and which was supported by people very similar in ideology, if not so elevated socially, as Coubertin. One of these men was Willibald Gebhardt, a chemist from Berlin, who read of Coubertin's ambitions for the Olympic Games and was determined to be the first German member of the International Olympic Committee.[31] The emperor himself was keenly interested in sport, which helped to make some inroads into the class with whom he most often associated. William II was always eager for his people to make a mark in the world. The eldest son of Chancellor Hohenlohe headed a commission to assemble a team of athletes. Then the German plans were balked by a brouhaha which, whatever its immediate origins might be, was ultimately due to Coubertin's reputation as a *revanchard*. A Paris newspaper, *Gil Blas*, had published on June 12, 1895, an interview with Coubertin in the course of which he boasted of the distinguished persons who had been at his congress a year before. There had been, he said, broad international representation: "Only Germany, which—perhaps on purpose—was invited very late, frowned at us and refused to take part in the congress." Furthermore, Coubertin stated, the Greek royal family was on bad terms with the Hohenzollerns and "their sympathies were French."[32] These provocative remarks were noticed and reported in a German journal for physical educationalists.[33]

The influential *National-Zeitung* did not pick up these tidbits until December 24, 1895. When they were published they ignited a blaze of editorials in the German press. Coubertin sent a denial of the charges to the *National-Zeitung*. He also proposed that the Germans suggest a candidate for a position on the International Olympic Committee who would then step in "when a vacancy occurred." On January 3, 1896, the *National-Zeitung* commented on this and other examples of "insolence" in Coubertin's letter. The ruckus grew and spilled over into

Athens where the games were scheduled to open in less than three months. Members of the Greek and German royal families, ministers, and sports bureaucrats demanded explanations or apologies from Coubertin, the newspapers, or each other. And, naturally, the turners set their faces resolutely against the Olympic Games.

5

ATHENS GETS READY

S HORTLY AFTER THE "Congress of the Sorbonne" ended
in late June, 1894, Bikelas, the Greek member of Coubertin's "International Olympic Committee," left for Athens. Less
than two years remained until the scheduled first meeting of the
modern Olympians was to open. Bikelas wrote reassuring letters
to Coubertin in Paris. All the Greek people as well as the royal
family joyously greeted the prospect of Olympic Games in
Athens in the spring of 1896. Coubertin himself rushed about in
Paris collecting data for the Greeks. He sought out and
conferred with the heads of various constituent bodies of the
Union de sociétés françaises des sports athlétiques. At the
time, a reason for national and even local chauvinism in sport
was the anarchy that prevailed in the regulations for play and
the standards for judging. So experts presented Coubertin with
their standard distances for various foot, cycle, and swimming
races, schedules of point systems for fencing, wrestling, and
gymnastics, and other instructions for judges and coaches.
(Coubertin thus, incidentally, assured that the feebly established rules then prevalent in Paris would gain a foothold not only
in the virgin territory of Greece, but in cosmopolitan sport generally). All was going well.

Then Coubertin received a less cheerful note from Bikelas
dated October 5, 1894, which said that the Greek Prime
Minister, Charilaos Tricoupis, "would have preferred that the
whole affair had never come up in the first place." Moreover, it

was "absolutely necessary" for Coubertin to come to Athens, for
his "presence" would "better facilitate things."[1] Coubertin
assembled his files and packed his bags. Before leaving Paris
he got out one of his trump cards, a letter from Franz Kemeny,
the Hungarian member of the International Olympic Committee, stating that Budapest would be prepared, even eager, to be
the host city for the Olympic Games in 1896. The festivities
could figure as part of that year's celebrations marking the
thousandth anniversary of Hungary's founding.

Coubertin took the fast train to Marseille and boarded the
steamer *Ortegal.* The ship sailed through the Straits of Messina,
south of the Peloponnesus and arrived at Piraeus, the port of
Athens, on the evening of November 8. Bikelas met Coubertin
at the gangplank the next morning and handed him the
duplicate of a letter addressed to the baron in Paris and dated
November 1. The purpose of the letter was to forestall the four-
day voyage just completed. It was from Stephanos Dragoumis, a
politician and a prominent member of the "Zappeion Commission" (named after the athletic foundation established in the
1850s by the Zappas brothers) which was charged with considering international games for Athens. The long letter was
graciously complimentary to the advanced ideas of the address-
ee, but gravely noted that Greece felt "an extreme reserve"
about the Games, since the country was then suffering from a
severe economic crisis "with resulting complications in her
foreign affairs." Besides, at the time, there scarcely existed in
Greece "any accurate notion of what Coubertin had called
'athletic sports.'" Paris in 1900, when the Games could be part
of the Universal Exposition, would be more suitable. Therefore,
"aware of the feebleness of the means actually at the disposal of
the Greek people and burdened with the conviction that the task
is far beyond the available means," the officials who had
examined the proposals really "had no liberty of choice" and
were forced to reject the "generous offer" of the 1894 Congress
of Paris.[2]

That was that! Bikelas and his freshly arrived guest had little more to do but kill time. The air was crisp; the sun was shining. They hired a calèche, put the folding top back, and drove off to the capital to inspect some of the sacred sites of antiquity. Bikelas pointed out Turkish and Byzantine, as well as classical, monuments. Late in the afternoon they lingered at a declivity between two hills in the southern suburbs. It was the site of the old stadium of Herodes Atticus. Nearby were garbage dumps from which windblown debris caught on pricker bushes. The principal sounds were the clucks and shrieks from chicken coops nearby. Bikelas spoke of the contests and festivals that this valley had witnessed for centuries. The orange and purple rays of the late sun tinted the stone buildings of the modern city, the white marble of Acropolis, and the grey mountains beyond. In the darkness on the way back to the center of Athens Coubertin pondered deeply, mumbled some figures to himself, began several times to say something to Bikelas, and then declared that the price of the modern festival, including the installation of temporary seats at the old stadium, could cost as little as 200,000 drachmas.[3] Just 200,000 drachmas and Athens might once more offer the world her glory.

Coubertin learned from Bikelas that the most important figure opposing the Olympic Games was no less than the prime minister, Charilaos Tricoupis himself. In the histories of modern Olympism, Tricoupis has been portrayed as the dragon bested by that Saint George of nineteenth-century athleticism, the dauntless baron Pierre de Coubertin. Before giving an account of their combat, however, we must first review some modern Greek history. The country had little exportable wealth with the exception of the products of her olive trees and her vines—particularly currants, which were then encountering a more competitive market because of the recovery of French vines from the diseases of the 1870s. Greece did export people. Since the days of the city-states energetic Greeks had left to be merchants and entrepreneurs in other lands, from where, to be sure, successive generations of Greeks maintained sentimental and economic bonds with their homeland. Expatriates remitted small and large sums to the folks at home and returned for long sojourns.

In late Roman times the country became an impoverished backwater of civilization. She was a Byzantine province and then an occasionally rebellious Turkish province. A usual method of Turkish political punishment was the imposition of slavery, or, if the logistical problems of shifting populations were too great, massacre. The struggles against the detested Turks in the early nineteenth century were so destructive that many philhellenes must have long regretted the price Greece had paid for her independence. The revolution had begun in 1821. With the help of Europe's great powers, a small, pathetically ravaged Greece was declared entirely independent in 1829. Athens shrank to a town of about 10,000 inhabitants huddled about the base of the Acropolis. A rickety old building, formerly a Turkish customs house, was all that remained at Piraeus where the harbor had meanwhile silted in. Greece had a monarch, a prince recruited from the Bavarian royal family, and, after the internal revolution of 1843, a constitution and a parliament. Until the 1850s, however, Athens, the capital and largest city, was a town with few people. Only small fishing boats could use the port.

There was a popularly approved change of dynasty in 1863. The new "king of the Hellenes" was George I, a big-nosed, taciturn seventeen-year-old, formerly a Danish prince of the Schleswig-Holstein-Sonderburg-Glücksburg house. The beginnings of modernization and the entry of Greece into the European intellectual community date from about 1870. This quickening was due to a general worldwide economic expansion, which spilled over into Greece partly in the form of more tourism and larger remittances from Greeks abroad. However, too much of the state's finances were obtained by floating Greek government securities in the Berlin, London, and, most partic-

The Princeton juniors who were members of the first American Olympic team in Athens in 1896. Left to right: Albert C. Taylor, Francis A. Lane, Herbert B. Jameson, Robert Garrett.

James B. Connolly, the Harvard student who was the "first man to win an event in the new Olympic Games, 1896." He won the triple jump with 45 feet.

Robert Garrett poses with the discus he tossed for an Olympic victory. The discus is presently in a display case in the main gymnasium at Princeton University.

Corvin Knapp Linson's depiction of Athenian "local color." Some of the ruins of the ancient city can be seen in the background.

THE OPENING
OF THE GAMES.

APRIL 6. 189

Opening ceremonies with a sampling of the costumes
worn on the great occasion.

Orthodox priests on the front row of seats.
In order to widen the infield for modern
track events, the first row of the old
stadium had been drawn back and was
now above ground over a retaining wall.

ICAL GROUP.

DRAWN BY A. CASTAIGNE.   **MAKING READY.**

Castaigne's sketch of the atmosphere in the athelete's changing rooms. The rooms were underneath the stadium.

Linson's drawing of a Greek discus thrower, probably Gouskos (see p. 119).

Spectators at the hurdle race. The leading-foot-forward style had not yet been invented.

THE FINISH OF THE HURDLE RACE.
(Marathon Day.)

Curtis, the American, leading; Goulding, the Englishman, a close second.

A view of the stadium from the south at a climax of the festival in Athens in 1896. Note the crowds of people on the hills overlooking the stadium on the right.

"Venetian Night" in Piraeus, on "Marathon Day" (April 10, 1896). One of the many festivals that took place in and around Athens during the first modern Olympic Games.

An impression of Spiridon Loues's finish. The "local color" is good, but actually the infield was packed when the marathon victor entered the stadium.

Spiridon Loues, the Marathon victor, at the official awarding of the prizes, Wednesday, April 15, 1896.

Idealized victors during the parade around the track of the stadium, April 15, 1896.

A cartoonist for the BOSTON GLOBE *(May, 1896) interprets a banquet for the triumphant Harvard athletes, the first Olympic heroes of the modern age.*

ANCIENT ATHENS GREETS THE NEW THROUGH HER ATHLETES.

André Castaigne's idealized depiction of an American athlete at the entrance to the tunnel in the restored stadium of Herodes Atticus.

ularly, Paris bond markets. The country had unhappy political interludes under jingoist and thieving chief ministers, but the bad spells were relieved by long periods of careful, autocratic rule under other statesmen who sternly tidied up after a diplomatic humiliation or the failure of the currant crop.

An enduring quality—some would say a fault—of the Greeks has always been their enthusiasm. Coubertin summed them up: "Such an impulsive yet serious people! The Greek quits and then takes new heart again and again. He evades giving a promise. He loves compliments yet suspects the person who offers them."[4] As soon as the Greek man in the street heard that an international festival in the form of the Olympic Games could be had for Athens, he passionately wanted them. What a fine spectacle! What better occasion to present to the world the splendors of both ancient and modern Greece? What an opportunity to show the hosts of foreign visitors that the classic birthplace of culture was not, as irresponsibly claimed, now a land of swindlers, brigands, and knaves.

Tricoupis's opponent, with whom he had alternated in power since the early 1880s, was the excitable flag-waver and demagogue, Theodoros Deligiannes, out of power at the time, declared his enthusiasm for the Olympic Games. Alas, in the year 1894, Greek fiscal affairs had arrived at a particularly dismal point, largely as a result of the shortsighted use of large sums from bond issues floated abroad. A lot of money originally slated for public works had been diverted to military expenditures. There had been "leakages" in transferring money among politicians, financiers, high-ranking bureaucrats, and contractors. In the fifteen-year period before 1894, the cost of servicing the public debt increased five times over. Indeed, normal taxation was insufficient to cover just this fiscal burden, not to mention the essential regular expenses of a functioning state. Greek bonds had fallen to between twenty-five and thirty-five (from a par value of one hundred) on the Paris exchange. The raisin crop had failed in 1894. Inflation, that rare specter which haunted the nineteenth-century bourgeois, was under way. In short, Greece was bankrupt. It fell to poor Tricoupis publicly to acknowledge this horror to creditors abroad.

This was the Athenian political atmosphere as Coubertin installed himself in the colonnaded, garlanded and urned Hotel de la Grande Bretagne, the usual home in Athens for voyaging people of his class. The building was one of the first modern structures to decorate Athens and was imposing enough to have served in the 1840s as a temporary royal palace. After the baron had been there a few days, Tricoupis himself called on him. Coubertin was crisply elegant in costume and in manner; Tricoupis was amiable, but sad and firm. He smiled at the Frenchman's estimate of 200,000 drachmas. He thought it was too cheap. On the other hand, he thought any money was too much for a sumptuary undertaking. In any event, debate over the price was futile, for where would even such a small amount come from? Coubertin's suggestion for a special levy was turned down. Rhetorical appeals citing the pride of Greek youth, the curiosity of sportsmen throughout the world, and the dreams of the universe of philhellenes and of humanity itself only tickled the old statesman's sense of irony. Before leaving he handed Coubertin a treasury report: "Look at this. Examine and study this list of our resources at your leisure. You can only become convinced that it is quite impossible."[5]

The scrappy Frenchman shifted the battle to a new front. Two days after his meeting with Tricoupis the newspaper *Asty* printed an open letter by Coubertin with the following observation: "We have a proverb which says that the word 'impossible' is not French. Someone told me this morning that the word is Greek but I didn't believe him."[6] The little fighter dashed about Athens depositing his cards and quoting the enthusiasm of cab drivers and shopkeepers to bank presidents and the chairmen of athletic and literary clubs. The alternative offer of the Hungarians was sometimes pulled out to be held in the palm of Coubertin's left hand and slapped with the back of his right hand. At a large assembly called by the literary society of Parnassus, he publicly reduced the price to 150,000 drachmas.[7] As was customary in his speeches during these years, the sportsman attributed much of the revival in sport to Englishmen. But Coubertin shifted the responsibility for continuing the sports renaissance to the Greeks themselves, who were told at the close of one speech:

> You will not be dishonored if foreign athletes defeat your Greek entries. A more serious defeat for you would be not to have struggled at all. In working for sport, be assured that you work as well for your fatherland.[8]

At the time, King George, now 49, was off in Russia for the funeral of the Emperor Alexander III. However, Coubertin had support from the crown prince, Constantine, Duke of Sparta, and his brother George, both of them boisterous giants well liked by the people. Coubertin and Constantine kept each other posted of the maneuvers of persons on the other side of the controversy which, within a week after Coubertin's arrival, had become the reigning topic of conversation in Athens. Once, Coubertin recalled later, while dodging some carriages in the middle of the city he glanced up at the Acropolis to see the gleaming, majestic Parthenon. It was as close as ever he got to this symbol of the ancient Greek spirit.[9]

He won more and more allies. Public opinion was on Coubertin's side. Two weeks after he had arrived in Athens, he squeezed from Tricoupis a promise of "benevolent neutrality" and the use of the Zappeion as a place to hold a rally. Using a familiar technique, Coubertin convinced Constantine to take the presidency of an "organizing committee," which of course Coubertin himself selected and convened. The sluggish members of the new committee accepted the dogged Frenchman's estimate of finances, his program of modern athletic events, lists of equipment, sets of international rules, and his sketches for a restored stadium and a modern velodrome. Then, suddenly, it was time for the promoter to depart. He had to return to Paris for, among other things, his marriage. He had been in Athens three weeks. On his way back, he took a morning off for a whirlwind tour of ancient Olympia, which seems not to have made a specific impression for he left no accounts of what he saw there at the time.

Perhaps the activity and undisguised comtemptuousness of the resourceful young Parisian (for Pierre de Coubertin was just thirty-three when he was in Athens) had been intimidating and had engendered a balky resentment while he had been on the scene. In any case, just after his departure, torpor, the reigning mood in the organizing committee, evolved somehow into euphoria—assisted, it must be admitted, by the repeated purgings and reorganizations by the diligent crown prince. The royal family was able to maneuver more effectively when Tricoupis resigned as prime minister (for reasons only partly connected with this dispute) in January, 1895.[10] Deligiannes, who took greater heed of public opinion, once more headed the government.

Newly appointed commissions rushed to arrange for the recruiting of a Greek team, the proper reception of foreign spectators and athletes, and the construction of suitable athletic facilities in Athens. Newly found Greek "experts" also planned for the various parts of the program for the prospective Olympic Games. There were to be track and field competitions, gymnastics, marksmanship, swimming, wrestling, fencing, cycling, tennis, sailing, and some cultural events. The Greeks later tampered with Coubertin's conception of field events and added events for track bicyclists and for fencers. They also dropped equestrian sports. This deletion nettled Coubertin, since he not only loved horses but had in January, 1895, already published and distributed a program of the Games that included jumping and trick riding. The experts charged with that part of the program explained that suitable breeds of horses did not exist in Greece and that there was no place to hold the events, though the Frenchman had boldly scheduled the horses and riders for the gymnasium of the cavalry school.

Pierre de Coubertin helped from Paris. He convinced the noted sculptor Jules Chaplain (1839–1909) to design the silver and bronze medals (gold, which stank of vulgar gain, was banned in the first modern Olympics). Puvis de Chavannes, the painter of the "Sacred Grove" in the great hall of the Sorbonne, a lover of antiquity, and one of the most respected academic artists of his time, agreed to design the award certificates. Coubertin recalled:

He appeared several times at my home to examine the drawings and photographs I had brought back from Greece. He repeatedly asked me questions, questions I could not answer, about the essence of "Greek lines," which was odd, since he had already so brilliantly perceived them and rendered them in his work. Finally, he wrote me that with great regret he was giving up the job, though he would have liked to have done it, since he found himself incapable of immersing himself sufficiently in the spirit of ancient Greece! Consequently the certificate was designed by some Greek who, fearing to plunge too deeply into the classic, abandoned himself to a sort of bizarre modernism. [11]

Coubertin searched Paris for the design of a velodrome he might copy, only to learn that Prince Constantine had independently obtained the plans for a steeply banked bike track he had seen once in Copenhagen. The baron also induced a travel agency in Paris to arrange a tour to the Olympic Games with one of the French steamship companies: three hundred francs for a first-class return passage from Marseille to Piraeus on the Senegal, which would stay in Piraeus from March 29 to April 13, 1896—the period scheduled for the festival. It was Coubertin who sent out the official invitations for the first revived Olympic Games (along with the first copies of his new *Bulletin du Comité international des Jeux olympiques*) to all the constituent bodies of his international organization. Aware that the Parisian was doing all the inviting, the Athenian hosts pressed him for estimates as to the numbers of foreign athletes and tourists they might expect. Coubertin could have furnished guesses, but he purposely withheld them since "Athenian expectations were growing daily and hardly at all accorded with reality."[12]

Greek expectations had been altered by financial events. Just after Coubertin left, Prince Constantine realized, as the Frenchman had, that financing would have to be done entirely apart from the national fiscal system. Though the government was financially paralyzed, it was able to help to the extent of authorizing a set of commemorative postage stamps (Coubertin had favored this over Greek proposals for a lottery) and exempting all tickets and gate receipts from taxation. Constantine would make a patriotic appeal for offerings from the Greek people at home and, through her consulates, Greeks abroad. By February 19, 1895, Timoleon Philemon, a former mayor of Athens and now the "Secretary General" of the Greek Olympic Committee (his title was traceable to the plan left behind by Coubertin), could write to the mastermind in Paris that 130,000 drachmas had already been subscribed. As a result of appeals made through the consulates, heavy donations were pouring in, particularly from the Greek communities in London, southern France, and Egypt. He also hinted at an impending windfall. Philemon had, in fact, dispatched a personal emissary to call on the richest Hellene in Alexandria, George Averoff, a shy businessman. Averoff had already quietly given Athens a technical school, a military academy, and a reform school. These rosier financial prospects made the Greek organizing committee open to suggestions that they restore the decrepit Panathenaic stadium. Members of the foreign academies, Germans especially, urged that the old stadium of Herodes Atticus be rebuilt, not temporarily with wood but permanently in the same gleaming marble from Mount Pentilicous that had originally faced it. Archaeologists and scholars even urged that approximations of the statues and bronze ornaments of ancient times be recast and remounted. Anastas Metaxes, a Greek architect who was already in the process of drawing plans and setting a schedule, guessed that a healthy beginning would cost about 200,000 drachmas (the drachma, it should be remembered, was originally equal in value to the French franc; it had decreased in value in the previous few years from about five to the dollar to about nine to the dollar in 1896). In Alexandria, Averoff was told that the total price would be 585,000 drachmas—and after a sales talk which, we can be sure, evoked the selfless benefactors of ancient Greece and very likely Herodes Atticus himself, the philanthropist declared that he would underwrite the whole cost. Later, when the restorers decided to use a high standard of workmanship and materials (evident to the visitor of today) and the bill came to just under a million drachmas, Averoff opened his purse yet wider.

This gift freed the organizers to use in other ways the funds originally set aside for the stadium. The dramatic force of the big donation also tipped a few more, wavering, potential benefactors. Eager architects, contractors, and construction bosses were unleashed to build a new gallery to shelter the contests in marksmanship and to build the velodrome, tennis courts, and facilities for the swimming meet. Still there was cash for evening festivals, fireworks, banquets, street decorations, theater, and music. A special budget provided for some new paving, installations of gas lights, and general sprucing-up in Athens. Officials, ushers, starters, and judges could be paid. There was even a surplus available for "leakage" when the money changed hands: bribery and suspicious bookkeeping were detected early in the selling of seats at the restored stadium. [13]

The Greeks were enchanted by their highly colored but insubstantially formed vision of what the Games might be and what they might produce for the nation. The country had little more than two million inhabitants at the time; Athens, by far the largest city, had about 135,000 and the Piraeus about 40,000 people. A large proportion of these individuals had participated in the civic generosity that had produced the financing, and many were working to beautify their city for the projected hordes of foreigners. Excited anticipation gripped the city. By the summer of 1895 a common evening excursion for Athenian families was to take a stroll in' order to gauge the pace of the reshaping and refacing of the ancient stadium.

During the later periods of Byzantine rule, the magnificent stadium of Herodes Atticus suffered from the gangrene that wrecked most marble monuments during that dismal time. The stadium became a quarry for rude, inferior buildings and for the lime furnaces that made the essential ingredient for mortar. Several times in the eleventh and twelfth centuries, however, crusading knights temporarily living in the ancient city used the still-level field for jousting tournaments. A fifteenth-century manuscript now in Vienna tells of the continued emplacement of many rows of white marble benches and the porticos above the sphendone. The pace of destruction, however, stepped up under the Turks when Athens, the seedbed of Western genius, slipped from the embrace of Western civilization. Excavators in the nineteenth century found the remains of four lime kilns near the sphendone and another near the old tunnel. The ovens were grim testimony to the fate of the white stone of happier days. Near one oven was found a fine, though mutilated, female head with a scrap of drapery attached and piece of a sculpted breast partly covered with the same drapery—evidence that precious statues were dragged whole to the oven and broken up before being fed piece by piece to the dissolving flames. Once the marble was gone, rain washed down the soil, restoring, over the centuries, the rugged outlines observed by Lycurgus.

Between 1869 and 1878 young King George himself paid for some excavations among the brambles and chicken coops. These diggings turned up pieces of sculpture in the style of the fifth century. Archaeologists discovered two fine mounted heads of Hermes that were turning posts in the old, narrow arena. Also uncovered was an unexpectedly large number of intact slabs of the original marble. They had long been beneath the surface and so were hidden from the Turkish lime burners. The slabs and blocks, slimy from algae and yellowed with age, were portions of flooring, walls, benches, and partitions. These indicated with some precision the dimensions and the layout of the old stadium.

The Athenians of the second century A.D. took four years to embellish their ravine. Upon receipt of the news in February, 1895, that Averoff would pay for a restoration, the Athenians had little more than a year to accomplish it. More than five hundred men were hired to right the damage caused by centuries of neglect and exploitation. The quarries of Pentilicous were mined again to turn that gulch into a white, classical stadium. There were day and night shifts. Still, by March, 1896, the task was far from completed. Near the bowled end the marble seats were completed up to the halfway mark; in the rest of the stadium there were many places where they only reached four rows. Restoration of the monument would resume after the Games, but most of the spectators in 1896 would sit on wooden benches.

The new stadium differed from its ancient model in that the stadium sports area or floor was made wider by moving the first row of seats back behind the retaining wall. This was a compromise demanded by modern footraces, which require curves for the runners. Minor additions included special thrones of white marble for the king and queen. The two rediscovered heads of Hermes and a life-size statue of Averoff were placed before the entrance to the new stadium. Acclaimed as the reincarnation of Herodes Atticus, the benefactor of 1,600 years earlier, Averoff, the modern philanthropist, was depicted in the costume of the late nineteenth century: draped tubes of cloth for the legs, buttoned boots, and a heavily padded, lapeled, double-breasted, tailed frock coat. The sculptor laboriously incised the details of the rich man's long hair and his full beard.

Facilities for the athletes were good. The old tunnel for beasts had been cleared and now led to lockers and changing rooms

with showers. The broadened track itself was still rather sharply
turned and the curved ends were not banked. An English expert
imported for the purpose had prepared the cinder track. In
March of 1896 the cinders were loose, because the track did not
have enough time to settle and "mature."

The Zappeion of the 1850s was in good condition. To its halls
were added a long, raised dais for the competitors and some
temporary stands for the spectators of the fencing matches. The
hall for workmanship was a new building at the Kallithea. As
the official report boasted, it was decorated "in the elegant style
of the late Renaissance." The velodrome was at New Phaleron
between Athens and Piraeus. The steeply banked ring for the
wheelmen had a circumference of one-third of a kilometer.
Coubertin was one of several who remarked on the irony that the
most fin de siècle of all the sports would be in the front rank for
a festival held in the most classical of landscapes. Some uneasy
and historically minded promoters of the new Games rational-
ized that the cycle races were surrogates for the chariot races of
antiquity. [14]

The new tennis courts were near the columns of the temple of
Jupiter. Coubertin's instructions for the swimming events (about
which he cared little) were the least specific and did not allow
for the numbing temperatures of the Mediterranean in early
spring. The notion of a heated swimming pool had penetrated
neither France nor Greece. The swimmers were to meet at the
little bay of Zéa at Piraeus. Distances were marked by the
spacing of barges large enough to hold starters, judges, the
contestants, and, in one case, a small band. The shooting
gallery, the tennis courts, the velodrome, and the bay of Zéa
were all provided with trellised and crenelated wooden pavil-
ions for the elevation, shelter, and proper framing of royalty.
These fussy architectural exercises were very up-to-date.

At some time during the late summer of 1895, the Hellenes'
self-confidence acquired a self-reinforcing momentum. Some
even adopted the romantic notion that the coming Games of
1896 were inspired by Greeks from beginning to end. More or

less unaware that he was being denied the gratitude he deserved, Coubertin continued to try to see that the athletic festival would indeed be international.

Coubertin recruited most diligently within continental Europe. We remember that the Hungarians had themselves offered Budapest as a site of the revived Olympics. To send a "Hungarian" team to an international at this time was, of course, a rather strong assertion of Hungary's independence within the Habsburg empire. Franz Kemeny, Coubertin's friend of earlier athletic congresses, obtained government financing to send a team of eight men. Arriving three weeks before opening day, the young Hungarians were the first to assemble in Athens and, once there, performed innumerable acts of self-advertisement. Frighteningly healthy-looking fellows, they stuck their rib cages out and breathed audibly as they paraded about Athens. Cocky, high-spirited, marching three or four abreast, they drew admiring stares and even stopped traffic. The Hungarians wore their blue and white national colors in little ribbons on their lapels. Often when they rode together in a cab, their own little portable flag fluttered at the front of it. They posed with alacrity for group pictures. One memorable Magyar, though he posed in a jersey shirt and short tight trousers, wore black hose about his bunching calves that nevertheless required garters with little buckles just below the knuckled knees. The day before the Games opened the Hungarian team drew particular attention by depositing a giant wreath during the ceremony for the unveiling of Averoff's statue in front of the restored stadium. Their principal training seemed to have consisted of public strutting.

Coubertin's personal connections with Swedish physical educationalists produced far less dramatic results. Captain Viktor Balck wrote that the Swedes were interested, but in the end the only Scandinavian competitor to make any mark was one Jensen, a cheerful weight lifter with striking blue eyes, short hair in a brush cut, and a neck so thick that all remarked about it.

Those who knew of Coubertin in the Low Countries distrusted

him. He could not recruit there. In any case the Dutch were known for their rigid definition of "amateur." They would have required that each competitor personally pay his way to the Games and all his expenses while there. The Belgians swore allegiance to their own particular ideas of what gymnastics should be. Here Coubertin's invitation aroused real enthusiasm, but it was all negative. The Belgians even sent around their own circulars damning any projected international games.

The composition of the French "team" suggests that Coubertin actually had little influence within French sporting circles. The spokesman for organized French marksmen found it quite inconceivable that some international committee could, even briefly, consider the Union des sociétés de Tir as a part of their polyglot organization. Coubertin encountered laughter in governmental circles when he proposed a subsidy for the expenses of some prospective French competitors.[15] What was called the French team consisted of two cyclists, some fencers, a runner, and a couple of French tourists with amateur credentials who happened to be in Athens in the spring of 1896. We can note here that the only other Latin who appeared primed for the struggles was a solitary Italian, Carlo Airoldi, who walked the 1,500 kilometers to Athens from Milan to get into shape and who, since he had no amateur credentials, was declared ineligible immediately upon his arrival.

In the meantime, the dispute among the German turning societies over the Olympic Games went on. A repeated argument against an international competition was that turning was entirely different from sport, which was an abstract, vain activity. One theorist wrote:

Our goal is to strengthen the spiritual and physical health of the entire German nation. . . . On the other hand the goal of sport is solely the reaching of peak performance [*Hochleistungen*].[16]

Some German classicists who favored German participation

in Athens stressed the strong spiritual connections between the modern Germans and the classical Greeks. They were encountered by those who stated that the classical Olympic Games were not cosmopolitan but exclusive. The turners recalled further that "Turnvater" Jahn saw turning as a means to dedicate oneself to the fatherland and that the enemy of the fatherland was always France. And the invitations to the Athens Games had come from the French patriot, Baron Pierre de Coubertin, who stood condemned in the turners' journals and in the German press.

Time was running out. In Berlin, Dr. Willibald Gebhardt corresponded with Coubertin and assembled a distinguished German Olympic Committee whose members were supposed to send an impressive German team to Athens. Gebhardt had some well-placed support in William II himself. Prince Constantine of Greece was married to Sophie, the emperor's sister. The Greek ambassador in Berlin repeatedly stated that the new Olympic Games, like the old, were Greek and not French. Gebhardt asked for and finally got a much desired telegram from Timoleon Philemon, the secretary of the Greek organizing committee, saying that "the President of the Hellenic Committee is the Crown Prince. The committee is independent with regard to everything regarding the celebration of the Athens Games."[17] This permitted some potential German Olympians to behave as though Coubertin never existed and that his preparations in Paris had never occurred. In late January, 1896, however, Gebhardt was still pressing Coubertin to delay the Athens Games until the autumn by which time he might recruit a large, first-class German team.[18] We can be sure that the prospect of German domination of the first modern Olympics did not cheer Coubertin up, but by this time he was powerless to influence much in Athens anyway.

Thwarted in Paris, Gebhardt hastily recruited three track and field athletes and ten turners from clubs in Berlin. The German

Olympic Committee was then attacked because few of the athletes were distinguished performers. Gebhardt, the athletes, and some officials left for Athens on March 21, 1896.

The campaign in Athens to squeeze out Coubertin had, by this time, gone far. Greek pride in their coming international festival was most important here. The efforts of the Greeks to strengthen the German organizers, and the Germans' efforts to soothe the patriots at home, also required that the Frenchman's contribution be minimized. Eventually the German Olympic committee sent Coubertin a conciliatory message expressing a wish for "the success of the common effort." Only on February 7, 1896, did Philemon, the patriotic head of the Greek Olympic committee, send Coubertin a telegram which (in clumsy French) declared, "The Hellenic Committee never believed the words attributed to you, founder of the renaissance of the Olympic Games." A warmer letter followed. [19]

When Coubertin turned up in Athens late in March, the organizers on the spot cast him in the role of just another journalist. Some of the laggards he had stirred in December 1894 now declined to recognize him. At a banquet where Coubertin happened to be present the tall Crown Prince gave the neglected Frenchman a significantly fervent handshake as he looked deeply into the little man's eyes, but that was as far toward civility as Constantine could go. There were angry objections in the patriotic Athenian press after several journalists learned that the correspondent in Greece of the *Temps* of Paris had referred to Coubertin as the restorer of the Olympics. With the sang froid of the intriguer whose goals have somehow been met, Coubertin later claimed he admired the Greeks' pride and felt no bitterness. [20]

In the light of the emphasis given in the program to sports that were established only in Anglo-Saxon countries, any schemes to recruit balanced, representative teams from the continent were perhaps foredoomed. One English observer remarked at the time, "Every nation except England and

America is still in an absolutely prehistoric condition with regard to athletic sports."[21] Only at the universities and in clubs for the upper classes of these nations was there an established range of athletic activities that could comfortably fit into the Games in Athens, the program for which was still essentially Coubertin's conception. What there was of organized sport on the continent was in the control of suspicious, warring clubs. Except in Germany and Scandinavia, the clubs were isolated from the state-supported educational systems which might have lent an existing organizational network and, conceivably, cash to build national teams.

Coubertin's many acquaintances in high places were unable to help him in England. The British sports officials to whom Coubertin wrote had no entry into Cambridge and Oxford athletic circles. This was particularly unfortunate since the universities' Easter holidays coincided with the time set aside for the 1896 Games. Due to an oversight of a kind particularly nettlesome to Englishmen, the official rules and program that Coubertin sent out were printed in French and were followed by (yet worse) a German version. It was only just before Easter that some private printer published an English invitation. But that invitation neither appeared to be nor was acknowledged to be official.[22]

The gap between British pride and the deference it was accorded resulted in a team of only six. But was this really a "British" team? One member, Goulding, was a hurdler who had earned a reputation at some meets in South Africa. Edwin Flack, a renowned distance runner, was in fact an Australian member of the London Athletic Club. A Mr. Boland of Christ Church, Oxford, happened to be in Athens at the time and entered as a British tennis player. Two young English employees at the British Embassy in Athens registered for the cycling events. Some of their offended countrymen caused a hubbub when they tried to bar these boys from the races. The cyclists were servants and thus could not possibly fit the English definition of "amateur." The youths did compete in the end, but the arguments preceding their participation made all Englishmen in Athens look ridiculous.

The Americans who appeared in Athens were the largest group of foreigners. Although in the early 1890s the United States was in its "athletic craze" and American competitive amateur sports were beginning to be nationally organized, neither the fad (for so it seemed to many) nor the organization directly influenced the Americans who went. American newspapers, a few of which were beginning to hire "sports writers" for "sports pages," scarcely noticed Coubertin's projects or the preparations in Athens. The head of the American Olympic Committee (so dubbed, as they all were, by Coubertin) was William Milligan Sloane, the popular professor of French history at Princeton. Sloane had a wide circle of influential acquaintances on the Eastern seaboard. In New York, however, Sloane had been unable to arouse any interest in the proposed revival of the Olympics.

Within the Princeton academic community he was more effective. Sloane arranged with his dean that four eager juniors could have six weeks off in the sprint to travel to Athens. They were Herbert B. Jameson, Francis A. Lane, Albert C. Taylor, and Robert Garrett. Given the university, the year, and the men's sympathies, it should come as no surprise to read that all were remarkably clean, clear-eyed youths who parted their hair down the center. Their trainer, "Scotty" McMaster, was prepared to travel with them. At the time, the American reputation of the Princeton track team was rather low. A writer in the *New York Times* observed:

Princeton may have a heavy surplus in its treasury, and the team may be in need of an ocean voyage. These are purely local questions. But the American amateur sportsman in general should know that in going to Athens he is taking an expensive journey to a third rate capital, where he will not even have a daily post from the outside world, where he will be devoured by fleas . . . , where he will suffer physical torments greater than at Saratoga Lake and where if he does win prizes it will be an honor requiring explanation. It is more than 2,000 years since the Greeks practiced the art of keeping their pores open by manly sport once a day.[23]

The most unusual-looking member of the Princeton squad was Garrett, the captain. He was of a Baltimore banking family. His mother had taken a palatial home at Princeton for the duration of the years her three sons would spend at the university there. Garrett, in fact, agreed to underwrite the expenses of the Princeton delegation. He was six feet two inches tall, taller than any other member of the American team. He also had rather oddly narrow shoulders from which hung two of the longest arms anyone had ever seen. He was a shot putter. On the schedule of events that Sloane had showed him he had seen listed as an event, "le lancement du disque." Some time before, library research suggested by Sloane had led the young lover of antiquity to have cast what he though was a reproduction of a classical discus. It was a slug of metal some twelve inches in diameter, an inch thick, and was, it developed, entirely unwieldy. Garrett forgot the matter.

Somehow Coubertin's circular announcing the projected international festival had reached some members of the well-heeled Boston Athletic Association, which had a good track team. The B.A.A.'s coach and trainer, John Graham, was born in England in 1861. He had taught athletics at Harvard when young and went to Germany in the late 1880s for more academic training in physical education. Upon his return Graham took his well-paid post as coach with the B.A.A.[24] Several of the men he had trained were record holders. That the B.A.A. should send some men to the Olympics was first proposed as a joke. At a meet in Mechanics' Hall in January, 1896, Arthur Blake, after winning the 1,000 yards foot race, remarked, "Oh, I'm too good for Boston. I ought to go over and run the Marathon, at Athens."[25] These jesting heroics were overheard by Arthur Burnham, a stockbroker, who pondered the suggestion briefly and then offered to promote the financing of an expedition. Oliver Ames, then governor of Massachusetts, agreed to meet any deficit from his own purse. The final team from the B.A.A. consisted of William Hoyt, a pole vaulter; Blake; Thomas Burke, a sprinter; Thomas P. Curtis, a hurdler; and Ellery H. Clark, a high jumper. All but the last were Harvard Alumni. Clark was a Harvard undergraduate who got permission to go to Athens because of his high scholastic average. Another member of the American team was James B. Connolly of the Suffolk Athletic Club in Boston. Connolly, too, was a Harvard undergraduate, but he ranked low academically. When his dean advised him not to risk the trip, since he might not be readmitted, Connolly replied, "I am not resigning and I am not making application to reenter. But I *am* going to the Olympic Games, so I am through with Harvard right now. Good day, sir."[26] Two more Bostonians were the brothers Sumner and John Paine, both captains in the army who were to compete in marksmanship. Just before leaving they were all joined by Gardiner Williams, a swimmer who paid his own expenses. Later, some American cyclists who were in Athens wanted to join the team, but they could produce no amateur credentials.

The Princeton and the Boston groups first met at the piers of the North German Lloyd lines on the morning of March 2, 1896, in Hoboken, New Jersey. The send-off was noisy, but one had to listen carefully to distinguish the club yells from the customary shrieking on docks and ships before a transatlantic crossing. The Princetonians' best effort was a repeated "Rah! Rah! Rah! Tiger! . . . Sis! Boom! Ah! Princeton!" The Boston Athletic Association bellowed "B.A.A.—Rah! Rah! Rah!" three times, each time rapidly increasing the tempo and raucousness. A small group of fans on the dock also yelled themselves hoarse and one rasped to a reporter, "There go eight instead of eighty. Where are all the vaunted clubs that live on their amateur sporting reputations?"[27] Though some of the New York newspapers perfunctorily mentioned the usual muscular imbalance on the passenger list for this sailing, there were no journalists recognizable among the clacques sending the athletes off. An exception was S. J. Viasco, editor of the New York (Greek) *Atlantis*, who broke through the crowds with basketfuls of flowers and a corsage for each of the boys.[28]

As was expected of young men with their positions in society, they all traveled first class on the *Fulda*. At their disposal they had dozens of waiters, pages, and other minions. First class also meant enormous meals (with delicatessen in between), masked balls, and the comforts of deck chairs and heavy woolen robes. The trainers, however, prescribed austerity and arranged with the ship's captain that most of the second cabin deck would be cleared for regular workouts. The Princeton boys jogged, dashed, or practiced their field events in two sessions per day in heavy sweaters and light rubber-soled shoes (their spikes would have wrecked the holystoned planking). The B.A.A. team worked out once a day, but longer. Clark later recalled that as he practiced the high jump, the results of his leaps were rendered unpredictable by the rolls of the vessel.[29]

At Bremen, the Americans changed ships and then sailed through the English Channel and south to Gibraltar, where they sojourned a few days. They trained on the playing fields of the British officers. Once, while other sightseers rode in carriages, Blake trotted behind, practicing for the Marathon. Clark later recalled:

Blake, who possessed, together with a sense of humor, histrionic ability to a marked degree, would stoop and pretend to pick up coins from the dust behind the carriages, shouting delightedly the while. The small boys were easy victims; we from our carriages, did our best to encourage the deception; and Blake, pursued by the barefooted hunt, came gloriously along in our rear, producing an effect almost equal to the real Marathon which was yet to come.[30]

From Gibraltar the assembled team sailed to Naples to take a train across Italy to Brindisi. From there they took yet another ship to Patras, where they boarded a lurching train that slowly traversed the rest of the way to Athens. At the station the Americans were welcomed by bands and hundreds of curious, chattering athletic enthusiasts. Then all marched to the city hall. There they were greeted by the first of many gesticulated, presumably flattering, speeches—all of them, of course, incomprehensible. Though tired, the youths were eager to be liked. At the city hall and at some other ceremonies they let themselves be forced to break training and drain bumpers of resinated wine when told that it would be a gross breach of etiquette not to accept them.

It turned out that a number of American tourists had detoured from Italy, the Holy Land, or Egypt in order to view the unprecedented spectacle in Athens. A Hellenic entrepreneur had marketed little national flags for lapel wear and groups of businessmen from the United States could be easily identified by their stars and stripes as they discussed the New York stock market or arranged wagers on the results of certain contests. Support for the American presence in Athens came from the heavy cruiser *San Francisco* at Piraeus, as commanding Admiral Selfridge was prepared to give his officers and men generous shore leave.

In view of the small number of foreign athletes available for the welcoming ceremonies, it became clear that the great majority of the contestants would be Greek. The commission charged with recruiting a national team had inspired a whirlwind sporting craze that was little more than a year old. Sporting clubs had sprung up everywhere. Groups of boys at street corners strained to heave a shot that was far too heavy for them. In fields near villages *diskoi* would fleck the sky. In Athens a policeman might be forced to clear a corridor on the street for some *flaneurs* informally competing in the long jump. Many athletes were training twelve or more hours a day. The reputations of the British, Americans, and Hungarians were intimidating, but who could tell. There might yet be some triumphs ahead for the Greek athletes. In three events, at the very least, the Greeks had clear advantages. Defying the precepts of the French promoter of the new Olympics, they had insisted on the discus which figured so prominently in vase paintings and was the subject of Myron's "Discobolus." The modern Greeks had had discus contests in their earlier "Olympic Games." The Greeks even had two champions, Paraskevopoulos and Versis, who were currently locked in a battle for the record. Of the two, Versis was the popular favorite. He was tall and had a symmetrically rippled v-shaped back. At his much-observed practice sessions, which recalled the voyeuristic atmosphere of the *palaestra*, Versis drew gasps of admiration. With his grace and dignity, he appeared momentarily like that perfect youth observed at a perfect moment which was saved for all time by Myron two thousand years before. Versis consciously copied the stance of the "Discobolous" and was referred to by the admiring Athenians as "Hermes."

Another hero of the man in the street was charismatic Gouskos, the favorite in the shot put. Gouskos attracted stares because he was so burly. Famous for his strength, Gouskos, along with several other men in the navy, had been given sixty days leave in which to practice his specialty. On a field near the stadium his trainer would have Gouskos heave the sixteen-pound ball twenty or thirty times in a row. This he did with a grace that made him appear to be a reincarnation of a classical hero. His thick hide grew richly brown in the sun and set off his unusually big, white teeth which he showed freely in big grins. Gouskos became a sort of folk hero. As he worked out, he too attracted hangers-on who were fascinated by his heavily corrugated musculature and the sight of the release of his explosive power. Evenings, Gouskos held court at a cafe on Constitution Square in the center of the capital. There he downed glasses of wine, waving at those who stared and roaring with the rich laughter that was expected of him.

A third focus for the Greeks' ambitions was the "marathon"

race. We should note again that until 1896 the contest was unknown as a sporting event. In the nineteenth century the most usual distance race at a track meet was 1,500 meters—and possibly as long as three miles for a cross-country or a steeple-chase, though there were records for longer distances. Still, the Greek committee charged with building a Greek team searched the country for men famed for endurance. Trials were held in the fall of 1895 to select the competitors for the forty-kilometer distance. For this even the Greeks also had a favorite, Vanitekes, who had won several practice runs. He smiled and nodded to acknowledge the applause that greeted him as he trotted on his workouts along the dusty, rocky road between the plain of Marathon and Athens.

As might be expected of the preparations for a spectacle that they hoped would lift their international reputation for fair dealing, the Greeks were honest in their relations with foreign athletes. However, their keenness for victory in the marathon led them to hold a late trial for this event, as the officials wanted to accommodate a couple of Greek runners who had been improving sharply. Their observations of the powerful strides of the Australian, Flack, had led them to this, an exceptional case of equivocal sportsmanship.[31]

As opening day approached, it was clear that Athens had not looked so handsome in centuries. The main streets had floral arches, flags, and shields bearing the legend "O.A." (*Olympiakoi Agones*—Olympic Games). Special garlands and banners decorated the parks of the city. Private citizens draped bunting of the national colors on the balconies of their houses. Money was provided to pay the wages of the musicians in the dozens of local and provincial bands. There was money to pay the necessary ushers at the sites of the contests as well as to compensate the officials who served on the organizing committees. The official reports have recorded the names of many of these officials: Colonel George Papadhiamandhopoulos was an athletic talent scout, Mr. Dimitrios Antonopuolos was scheduled to judge the shooting events, Mr. Yenissorlis reviewed the entries for the track and gymnastic competitions, as did Mr. Colocotronis those for fencing.

The older royal princes, Constantine and George, influenced many of the festivities. As was noted earlier, due to the bankruptcy of the state treasury the Games were financed and organized independently of the government. In the Greek constitution, royalty was denied a role. At first sight, it might appear that the new Greek Olympics were similar to the ancient Olympics which were held on politically neutral territory. In fact, however, the royal family managed to insinuate itself not only into the preparations, but into many of the ceremonies and events as well. Before opening day the tightest scheduling was devised to assure widespread and repeated formal appearances by the king, the queen, the five princes (the younger three princes—Nicolas, Andrew, and Christopher—did little except wave), and the princess Marie with her fiancé, Grand Duke George Michailovich of Russia. The royal family reserved the best horses and carriages for rapid movement from one center of activity to another. Despite the demand for fervent, contentless speeches and rapid changes of attire, the taciturn king, the two older princes, Marie, and the Grand Duke all stood the pace. The queen, however, became indisposed halfway through the proceedings—just after she had opened the marksmanship competitions with a shot from a pistol draped by garlands of tiny flowers.

In the meantime, almost no Greek expressed even gentle disapproval. The good-humored Athenians accepted the disruptions in routine in their city without any of the complaints or wisecracks typical of critical sporting spectators, for this kind of festival was entirely novel to them.[32] A further reason for high spirits in Athens was that the Games occurred during the Easter season. In the Eastern or Orthodox church, Easter, marking the resurrection of Christ and the victory of life over death, is a holiday of great importance and considerable gaiety. In 1896,

Easter Sunday was April 5 (or March 24 on the calendar observed by the Greeks until May, 1923), which coincided with Easter Sunday in the West. Vendors in the market sold the traditional lamb for the holiday meal. There were religious parades on the streets and special masses in the cathedrals. People greeted their friends with the traditional "Christ is risen!" and were answered, "Christ is truly risen!" Although most Athenians were clad in the rustling and padded dark clothes demanded at the time, the dominant public mood was one of joyful expectation.

On Easter Sunday there was a ceremonial unveiling of the statue of Averoff, whose generosity had made the lavish presentation of the Games possible. Because of the rain and cold winds many in the crowd carried umbrellas, but ranks of army regiments and court officials stood bareheaded at dripping attention throughout the speeches. Curiously, the shy Averoff refused the invitations to be a guest at the Games. Another curious situation, much observed and commented on, was the close association of the bearded Metropolitan of Athens in his black robes and Père Didon, who was dressed in the white prescribed for the Dominicans. They were often together during subsequent athletic contests. Both were called on for appropriately ecumenical prayers. Two major Christian faiths thus blessed the restoration of a pagan festival abolished by a Roman emperor who had determined that the Olympics were not consistent with Christian piety.

The opening ceremonies were scheduled for April 6, the day following Easter Sunday. The night before, the competitors—like all competitors whose trainers have ordered them to "get a good night's sleep"—twisted in anticipatory torment in their beds. Compulsively, ceaselessly, their hot imaginations led them to partially dreamed, heart-thudding previews of the struggles, at once eagerly awaited and grimly dreaded, of the next ten days.

6

THE ATHENS GAMES

*T*HE OPENING DAY of the Olympic Games in Athens in 1896 was also, coincidentally, the anniversary of Greek national independence, thus permitting a forceful and intimate mixing of religious, patriotic, and athletic enthusiasm. Early in the morning the royal family celebrated a *Te Deum*. Loyal subjects filled the cathedral and overflowed into the streets. Provincial bands played for the crowds moving along the boulevards leading to the stadium. A jarring note, however, was provided by scalpers who had bought up blocks of seats and were peddling them to groups at the stadium entrance.

In order to accommodate the streams of pedestrians, only the carriages of high dignitaries were permitted on the roads going to the stadium. Though joyously animated, the fans were docile, and special detachments of the Greek army easily maneuvered them to their seats after the gates opened at noon. By two o'clock all the places were taken and the bare hills rising above the stadium were covered with less prosperous locals who had shrewdly escaped paying the rather steep entrance fees. It is noteworthy that on this Saturday, April 5, 1896, the audience made up one of the largest groups of individuals to be assembled for peaceful purposes since ancient times. There was probably no gathering place in the world that rivaled the stadium of Herodes Atticus in it seating capacity of about 70,000 (estimates varied), and there were an additional 50,000 on the hillsides. Athens itself was nearly deserted. Curiously,

though, there was little burglary in the city during the festival.
Apparently the occasion had drawn thieves as well as honest
men to the stadium. The spectacle of the somber clothing was
relieved by the uniforms of the grouped musicians and soldiers
in the regiments. More color was provided by the raised flags of
the competing nations. They flapped in the air above the sphendone, the curved end of the stadium.

It was not until 3:15 in the afternoon that the royal family
arrived, the king in the uniform of an infantry general and the
queen—in contrast, with the rest of the ladies—in billows of
white. As the crowd stood at attention, the royal couple led a
procession consisting of their large family, ranks of ministers,
senior army and navy officers, bureaucrats, and, last, officials
of the various organizing committees. The king and queen then
took the oversized marble thrones of honor to sit on cushions of
red velvet. Surrounding them were diplomats and high ecclesi-
astics, among whom, side by side, were the Orthodox metropolitan and the Dominican tourist, Père Didon. When the music
of the royal hymn died down, Prince Constantine, with his
retinue, advanced to the center of the stadium and shouted a
speech of religious and patriotic clichés which almost no one
could hear. At the end of this, the king arose and announced, "I
hereby proclaim the opening of the First International Games in
Athens!" The crowds, seeing that something significant had
occurred, cheered. When calm was restored, all bands assembled in the center of the stadium, where they were joined by
supplementary strings plus a choir of three hundred voices, for
the "Cantata of the Olympic Games." Greeks wrote the music
and words:

Immortal spirit of antiquity—father of the true, beautiful, and
good—descend, appear, shed over us thy light upon this ground and
under this sky which has first witnessed thy unperishable fame.

Give life and animation to those noble games! Throw wreaths of
fadeless flowers to the victors in the race and in the strife! Create in our
breasts, hearts of steel! In thy light, plains, mountains, and seas shine

in a roseate hue and form a vast temple to which all nations throng to adore thee, oh immortal spirit of antiquity![1]

After the conclusion of the cantata's crescendo, the response of king and crowd was so enthusiastic as to require a second performance.

As the musicians retreated to their blocks in the stands, attention shifted to a group of about twenty youths at the stadium's tunnel. They were clad in light sleeveless shirts, shorts, and spiked running shoes. Each athlete bore a number sewn on his jersey. He could be identified from the program. It was already late. Someone blew a bugle and some runners jogged to their starting lines.

The first contests were the four preliminary heats in the 100-meter dash. The starts were rather messy affairs by modern standards. The sprinters were similar in that all had the deadly, determined looks of strong men armed from within for maximum effort, but their positions were various. Some were upright, with forward and backward clenched fists; some were in a tight semi-crouch; while the Americans introduced into international competition the hunkered heads-up position which later in the history of athletics would lead to the introduction of starting blocks. The non-Greek athletes attributed the poor times (as well as all later running performances) to the loose surface and hard base of the new track.

The next event, the triple jump (or hop, skip, and jump), had aroused some patriotic anticipation since the event had been known and performed in Greece and the two young Greeks who entered and appeared agile in practice. But the winner was Jim Connolly of Boston, whose final mark was more than a meter beyond that of his nearest rival, a Frenchman resident in Athens named Tufferi. The better of the Greeks was a close third. Not overly modest, Connolly, a frowning Irishman, had caused a sensation before his jump when, and after the best effort of Tufferi was pegged, he threw down his cap a yard beyond it. Had the audience known something of the existing records for the event, they would have been less astonished at this gesture—at once arrogant and joking. When Connolly actually leaped just beyond the cap, spectators sprang up shouting, "It's a miracle! A miracle!"[2] It was at the conclusion of this event that all present first saw the ceremony honoring the victors. A group of uniformed sailors were posted at a high flagpole at the entrance to the stadium. There, immediately after Connolly's victory was announced, the American flag, followed by Connolly's number, went rapidly to the top. All admired the sight, but the most enthusiastic were the robust American athletes whose bizzare college cheers for the first time astonished the closely packed Hellenes. "It is the yell of the wild Indians," some murmured.

Next came the preliminary heats for the 800-meter run. There were two heats of seven men each. Only the first and second places in a heat won the right to compete in the finals. In the finals, likewise, third place was not ceremonially acknowledged; thus the Athens Games can be considered an intermediate stage between the ancients who cheered only victors and the present Olympics which officially recognize third place.

Greeks performed poorly in the 800-meter run. The fans' interest then shifted to what was, for them, the most important event of the day. This was the discus throw, an event of ageless beauty revived by the Greeks from depictions in classical art and carefully prepared for only in Greece. In the darkening evening, the competing athletes were impelled to wear heavy coats or sweaters against the chill. The favorite was Versis, who, in form and in motion, was an almost lyrical evocation of classical harmonies.

Astonishingly, this event drew an international field of entries. There were several Greeks, three Danes, a German, a Frenchman, an Englishman, the lone Swede at the Games, and one American, Robert Garrett. Garrett was probably the only foreigner whose interest in the discus antedated the Games themselves. At Princeton he had briefly considered preparing for the event, but abandoned his discus since it was too heavy. While jogging about a practice field just after he arrived in Athens, however, Garrett had seen a dish-shaped object lying in the turf. He picked it up and, upon examining it, saw that it was made of a hard, tough wood with a small brass center and a protecting rim of wrought iron. By means of a short pantomime, a Greek athlete informed Garrett that he held a competition discus. It weighed just two kilograms, or about four and a half pounds. His teammates agreed that he might as well try it, so Garrett devised an individual style of wind-up for the throw. His technique differed from that of Versis, who took a little hop and then let go; Garret, instead, spun upward from a deep crouch and released the discus at the end of his abrupt, centrifugal motion.

His efforts were clumsy compared with those of the Greeks and were curious to observe. So were the approaches of the other foreigners. Each man was allowed three attempts; the longest throw would win first place. Wobbly arcs, flubs, and deep embarrassment quickly cut the original field of eleven down to three, Garrett and the two Greek stars. Versis, the slenderer and more nobly handsome of the natives, quit after his second try, which was lovely to watch but weak. In his third and last throw, Paraskevopoulos gave his all: it was the best toss of the day. At once he was the darling of the crowd who had never seen the discus sail so far or so evenly. Then came Garrett. He let flail his long arms with an effort that made him grunt piercingly. As the discus cut the air, the mass of cheering Greeks quieted at once. No! A tie! After some painful moments the measuring officials were forced to announce that Paraskevopoulos had been beaten by just nineteen and a half centimeters.[3] There was consternation in the stands as the Yankees did peculiar victory dances, embraced and slapped one another on the buttocks. As the Greeks recovered from their shock, their warm blessings gradually overwhelmed the briefly isolated jubilations of the victor's teammates. For the second time that day the stars and stripes flew to the top of the pole at the front of the stadium.

It was dark, cold, and gusty by then. The already dispersing crowds scarcely noticed the last events, the heats for the 400-meter run. Thousands of spectators were in the infield, but were orderly and warmly demonstrative as the first family left to the accompaniment of the royal hymn. The festive atmosphere continued into the evening. There were special illuminations of electric and gas lights in the center of the city and some torchlight processions.

On opening day attention had centered upon the events in the stadium. The next day, the royal family offered their presence to the opening of the fencing competitions in the colonnaded central hall of the Zappeion, since the 1850s a center for sporting activities. The fencing matches took place on a raised dais that was surrounded by temporary bleachers. Coping saws had been diligently applied to decorate a trellised, crenelated enclosure for the royal spectators. Bands played in the balconies. The fencers in the eleven preliminary, individual foil matches were French or Greek. The French fencers were in good form. The final match was between Gravelotte and Gallot, who took first and second places respectively. Gravelotte also later won the epée championship. Two days later, an Athenian university student, Georgiades, took the saber event amid rejoicing.

At the stadium on the second day the athletes performed before a rather sparse crowd of onlookers. Much popular curiosity had been satisfied and there was open dissatisfaction over the high admission prices. The preliminaries of the high hurdles opened the program. The novel performances appeared droll to the spectators. The practice runs gave rise to incredulous snickers. Nevertheless, among the contestants were four Greeks who would approach the barriers, hesitate, then spring, landing on both feet, and then going on to the next hurdle. The American, Bill Curtis, won one heat and, as expected, the renowned Englishman, Goulding, took the other. Goulding had previously strutted about Athens explaining the origins of the medals on his chest. Curtis later reminisced, "I never met a more confident athlete."[4]

Eighteen competitors had registered for the long or broad jump; eight appeared. But then the field was almost immediately cut to Ellery Clark of Boston and the hero of the previous day, Garrett. After a bitter struggle, with overtones of American intercollegiate rivalry, Clark won and once more the Greeks saw the American banner flap in the wind and heard the vociferous college hurrahs which were now quite consciously staged for the appreciative spectators. Immediately after this, in the final of the 400-meter race, Tom Burke of Boston barely won first place from his teammate, Herbert Jameson, who took second. Once again the familiar stars and stripes shot to the top of the standard in the stadium—so far the only national flag to be seen there.

By now the elation of the Yankee team was boundless. Their leaping, embracing, and cheering caused them to be viewed as entertainers apart from their physical prowess. An American victor was particularly admired when no Greek was closely beaten. Verging on giggles, but nonetheless respectful, the crowds went silent when the Americans began their robust chants—all the better to appreciate them. The little band of athletes were soon helped by the officers and men of the cruiser *San Francisco* who joined in "B.A.A.!" or "P-R-I-N-C-E-T-O-N! Rah-rah-rah!" locomotives followed by the name of the individual performer who evoked the cheer.

The fourth event of the second day was the shot put—another supposedly Greek event, just below the discus and the marathon in sentimental appeal. During the preceding year, young Greeks in their villages had spontaneously formed groups to heave the sixteen-pound weight competitively. But because of the reputation of the Greek champion, only seven of the fifteen inscribed entries started and these were quickly cut to two.

Which two? The crowd's hero was the bull-like (he was about five feet eight, but weighed well over 200 pounds), bearded, bronzed, laughing Gouskos.[5] Just before Gouskos's tosses, he would squat, coiled before the low barrier, and then with a spring and a spine-chilling bellow he would heave. Gouskos's opponent, Garrett, had also been training and, unlike Gouskos, took advantage of the seven-foot run allowed the competitors. At the end it was the American who was declared victorious, though by only a few centimeters. Then came a hideous muddle. The winning shot was Garrett's first, which he never again approached although Gouskos did. During these later throws the fierce, proud joy of the massed thousands was palpable. When the competition was declared over, the sailors at the flagpole, misled by the applause and sharing the general impression, shot up the banner and number they had at hand, those of the Greek hero. One can imagine the massed feeling of revulsion and despair when the error was speedily corrected. American joy and self-congratulation became, on the other hand, boundless. And after a while the crestfallen Greeks wistfully joined their mad rejoicing. The good-natured Gouskos, whose personal charm had touched even the youths from across the sea, became the subject of a gracious American cheer.

No American took part in the next event in the stadium, which must have been a relief. The weight-lifting competition was held on a circular, sanded area in the center of the field encompassed by the track. There were just two events in this part of the meet. Jensen, the Dane of marvelous neck, won the two-handed press (which was to become familiar in later Olympic Games). Second was Lawrenceton Elliott, an Englishman. Elliot also won the one-armed jerk. The English athlete was one of the traffic stoppers in Athens. As the official report of the Games noted, "This young gentleman attracted universal admiration by his uncommon type of beauty. He was of imposing stature, tall, well proportioned, his hair and complexion of surprising fairness."[6] The spectators were also some-what comforted, no doubt, to see the English and Danish flags at the top of the mast for a change.

During the weight–lifting a curious occurrence further endeared the royal family to the populace. A minor functionary labored over moving a weight no longer in use. Prince George, a man everywhere noticeable because of his huge size, picked up the weight and tossed it some distance, giving rise to gasps of admiration.

The final event of the day was the 1500-meter run. The victor was the Australian, Edwin Flack. Blake, the American, was a very close second. The finish had been tense because both had just barely pulled ahead of a short Frenchman named Albin Lermusieux. Lermusieux, the only French track athlete to make any showing at all, was one of the "characters" among the visitors. After he was introduced, an American asked him about his specialties. They were, he said, the 100-meter dash and the marathon. When requested to explain how he trained for this odd combination, he answered, "One day, I run a leetle way, vairy queek. Ze next day, I run a long way, vairy slow." When queried as to why he wore white gloves, the Frenchman replied, "Ah-ha! Zat is because I run for ze king!"[7]

Events were scheduled in several places in and around Athens on the third day, April 8. In the morning the king and queen inaugurated the shooting gallery at Kallithea. The first contest was for rifles at two hundred meters, but, though shooting went on the whole day, nothing was decided since there were 160 competitors (only ten of whom were foreigners). The tennis matches, held in a large, circus-type tent near the columns of Jupiter, were only eliminations for the singles and doubles. The tennis players were grateful to be shielded from the cutting winds of the coldest day since February. Snow covered Mt. Pentilicous. All contests scheduled for the stadium for April 8 were postponed.

Undaunted, the royal family, minus the queen (who needed a

rest), appeared at their jigsaw-gingerbreaded pavilion to inaugurate the velodrome with its circumference of one-third of a kilometer. The sole event of the day was a race of one hundred kilometers. Grim skies, plus the grim monotony of the spectacle, caused the few onlookers to lose interest rapidly after the first whirls at full speed. One by one the ten starters fell out until, long before the dizzying last laps, only a Frenchman, Flamand, and a Greek, Collettis, remained. Partly because of the dreadful weather, both cyclists looked nearly broken at the end. Flamand skidded and fell with much flailing just before the finish, but remounted quickly enough to win, whereupon he was carried moaning from the track. The persistent Colettis was eleven laps behind him.

On the fourth day, Thursday, the weather had scarcely improved but events went on in several parts of Athens anyway. The tennis eliminations continued. Two Greeks, Karassevdas and Pavlidhis, won the first and second places in rifle shooting at two hundred meters. However, the patriotism of the great mass of the locals was not aroused by these victories, nor by that of Georgiades who had taken the saber competition, for the thrilling flag-raising ceremony occurred only at the stadium.

In an attempt to combat predictions of sparse attendance, the royal family, minus the queen but plus the visiting king of Serbia, appeared at the stadium. The distinguished guests were greeted with the royal hymns of both Greece and her northern neighbor and there was another performance of the "Cantata of the Olympic Games." The only track event of the day was the final of the 800-meter run. The Australian, Flack, won in the creditable time of two minutes and eleven seconds. A Hungarian, Dani, took second.

Most of the competitions of Thursday, April 9, consisted of the gymnastic events. The Germans had sent a small squad, snappily dressed in their tight uniforms of white jerseys and gray trousers. There was also one Bulgarian and one Swiss, the sole representatives in Athens from their respective nations.

The Greek teams had practiced long and hard for these events, and they had perfected the elementary maneuvers. Their grace was much appreciated by the crowd. The Germans drew sarcastic comments becase they stood stiffly at attention before launching into their routines. Taking advantage of the scoring system, which awarded more points for courage and invention, they did the more difficult exercises well, but with frequent mistakes. Spectators hissed and gasped ("were not the Hellenes surpassingly beautiful?") as the black and white flag of Imperial Germany was hoisted for victories in the team parallel bars, the team fixed bars, and the long (horse) vaults. There were muted "boos" as the Greek audience displayed its ignorance of the recondite rules of turning competition. Zutter, the Swiss, watched the Swiss flag rise to signal his win in the long vault combined with rings, an exercise that has been rarely heard of since. Germans then went on to win the first and second places in the fixed bars. Then, perhaps sensing the eager yearnings of thousands of patriotic Greeks and the interest of kings and princes, two Greeks, Nitropoulos and Persakis, won first and second places in the flying rings. At last the Greek flag was raised at the stadium! The overjoyed mobs threw hats and handkerchiefs into the air and rejoiced in their first opportunity to wave the little blue and white Greek flags that they had been carrying for days.

Darkness required the postponing of the rest of the gymnastic events until the next morning, the fifth day of the Olympic Games. A few Greeks competed on the individual parallel bars, but were overshadowed by Alfred Flatow, a German. Then in the rope climb, Andriakopoulos, who was first, and Zenakis, who was second, triumphed over a small international field that included Hoffmann, the biggest and strongest of the Germans, Jensen, the Dane, and the large (six feet four) and fair Englishman, Elliot. Again all the spectators were delighted for the opportunity to greet the raising of the Greek flag as it announced the winners.

Americans won no victories on Thursday, for there had been no events they were prepared to compete in. On Friday, April 10, it was different. In the marksmanship competitions for pistols at five meters the winners were John Paine, first, and Sumner Paine, second. The Paine brothers, we recall, had traveled from Boston with the track men. The contest was quickly over for no one came near them in accuracy. The Greek official report attributed the victory to their personal guns "fabricated on a most superior system and endowed with remarkably correct aiming power."[8]

In the stadium on Friday the first track event was the final in the 100-meter dash. An American, Tom Burke, won the silver (i.e., first-place) medal. Hoffmann, a large German turner whose specialty was rope climbing, was a close second. Once again, the familiar American flag was raised. Then, just a few minutes later, with another upward flight of the stars and stripes, the peculiar hurrahs and "Zizz! Boom! Bahs!" of the Yankee youths took on a special ferocity. Tom Curtis had won the finals in the 100-meter hurdles from Goulding. The Englishman's tales of earlier triumphs in South Africa had led all Athens to share his view that he was the world's fastest hurdler, but he lagged in the first brief burst, gained on the leaps but lagged once more to dash through an already broken tape, "whereupon he stopped neither to linger nor to say farewell, but went from the stadium to the station and took the first train away from Athens."[9] In the meantime the high jumping had begun. Out of consideration for the two Greeks who jumped first, the bar was set low and moved up only a few notches at a time. Eventually three Americans—Clark, Garrett, and Jim Connolly—remained to fight out a rivalry between the Boston and Princeton factions of the team. When the American flag went to the top it carried the number of Clark from the B.A.A.

In the pole vault, again only Greeks and Americans competed. The impatient Ivy Leaguers waited as the bar was slowly eased up from a height so low as to be unnatural to them, since they were accustomed to greater heights. After a while the Greek youths dropped out to become keen spectators. They kindly massaged and kept limber the tense limbs of Hoyt and Taylor. They also supplied sugared hot drinks, for the weather had become so cold as to be almost numbing. Taylor was in the end the winner at a mark far below his previous personal best. For a while the spectators in the stadium had observed the brief sprints, the placed pole, and the graceful vaults, but the conclusion of the event and the subsequent raising of the familiar flag attracted almost no attention. More stirring events were taking place elsewhere. The first running of the marathon was nearing its finish.

Even more than the discus throw, this event, dramatically evoking past glories, seemed poetically apt for a major Greek effort.[10] Consequently, the committee recruiting a national team had made special efforts to develop distance men. During the winter of 1895–96, runners from several parts of the country could be seen chugging along the stony, rising and falling road and through the dusty hamlets between the plain of Marathon and the capital city. Some were shepherds who were urged to come forth because of their reputations for perseverance, some were soldiers who were the best of the distance marchers. As was mentioned earlier, the list of marathon entries was the only one that the Greek officials tampered with. Two weeks before the race, because of the strong and graceful running style of the Australian, Flack, they held a late qualifying race for Greeks. One of the late entries was Spiridon Loues of the village of Marousi.

The Greeks, upon learning that the first marathon was to be held on the occasion of their first international festival, were captivated by visions of victory. To the winner, should he be a Greek, businessmen in Athens offered cash prices or annuities (of course, strictly forbidden by the amateur rules) and such things as free restaurant meals for life. Tailors, hotelkeepers, barbers, and hatters made similar offers. On the day of the race, despite the continued high admission charges and the unseasonable cold, the stadium was actually overfilled by squeezing spectators closer together and by seating them in the aisles. The hills above the stadium were also covered with nonpaying onlookers. Thousands carried their little Greek flags, just in case. Besides the more than 100,000 observing the finish line at the stadium, the road from the start to Athens had lines of spectators and clustered masses in the villages along the route. In Athens itself, thousands were packed along the boulevards near the stadium.

Though there was a larger number of registered entries, just twenty-five men appeared the evening before "Marathon Day" to spend the night in an inn at the small town of Marathon. Several were foreigners, of whom Flack was the most feared. Other non-Greeks were the American, Blake, who had diligently trained for the event, a tall Hungarian named Kellner, and the chatting, gesticulating Frenchman, Lermusieux. Just before two o'clock all were placed two deep along the starting line. They gripped and ungripped their hands, coughed, stamped, and repeatedly replaced their spiked shoes. Several of the Greeks chewed on sticks of tough, fibrous wood. Mounted army troops behind the racers were to act as judges. There were also a few coaches on bicycles and a fully equipped horse-drawn hospital wagon with accompanying physicians. After his superfluous speech describing the forty-kilometer course, Colonel Papadiamantopoulos fired the starting pistol.

The race was odd from the beginning. Lermusieux, who was later accused of repeatedly sipping from a flask of brandy before the start, dashed to the lead and held it. At the village of Pikermi, some fifteen kilometers along the way, the Frenchman was three kilometers ahead of his nearest rival, Flack, who in turn was closely followed by Blake and Kellner. Farther back were three Greeks led by Lavrentis of Marousi (who, it was claimed the next day, had been an enemy of Loues, also of Marousi, from childhood). About midway through the race, rumors began to reach the stadium that, once again, no Greek had a chance. At the twenty-third kilometer, Blake fell and could not rise; it was later reported that before he fell blood could be seen coming out of his low shoes. Several Greeks who had kept pace with the leaders collapsed and were hauled, morose and tearful, into the hospital van. At the village of Karvati some excited peasants broke through the police lines to offer Lermusieux a victor's wreath as he ran under the flowered arch of triumph they had erected for the occasion. He took only some sugared wine to strengthen him for the long hill that rises to Athens. Then, just as fatigue fell like a sticky blanket on him, the Frenchman's cycle-mounted coach drew close to shout advice and accidentally bumped him. He fell badly. Bewildered, he rose and somehow plodded on.

Of course no one knew how to run this race—how to prepare for its appalling physiological and psychological demands. Flack's inexperience with such a distance over such terrain had led him also to panic because of Lermusieux's early pace. Flack had once passed Lermusieux before the Frenchman fell, then the Australian was passed, but took the lead again at the thirty-sixth kilometer. Then he was passed once more, whereupon he veered off the road and collapsed in a heap. Some said he was unconscious, some said he was raving as he was carried to the ambulance carriage. The long incline shortly before Athens, which knocked out the foreigners, benefited the well-trained natives. Though far behind the leaders, Spiridon Loues never lost confidence and rarely altered his rhythm. After his steady labor up the hill past Karvati he experienced that intense satisfaction—familiar to the patient, superior distance runner—of passing rivals who had not paced themselves properly. It appears that Loues worked a psychologically devastating trick on the leaders by slowly squeezing past them, then letting himself be passed, and the inching past again. Loues did this to Flack at the thirty-third kilometer and may have wrecked his will to go on. He likewise demoralized his nearest Greek rival, with whom he shared the lead as they neared the suburbs of Athens.

Lips were trembling, knees were shaking, hearts pounding, lungs expanding to such an extent that the wall of the chest seemed as if they would truly burst under the pressure; and with that was a stew of muscle, nerves, and flesh; as if the spinal column would dissolve and the stomach crumble in beside it; as if the eyes would melt in their sockets and the brain go mad for very aching; and down the face, neck and shoulders and breast and back, over every square inch of the body, ran streams of not mere summer sweat that was salty, but sweat that smelt of dissolving blood, that was maddeningly thirstful where it touched the lips and tongue.[11]

Once the shoulders of the rivals grazed each other. Then Loues, his face twisted with pain, pulled ahead and stayed there. A cannon boomed to announce the approaching victor. Young girls along the boulevards in Athens threw flower petals before the Greeks as girls in the villages had thrown them before the French and the Australian runners. Soon Loues was nearly hidden by screaming boys forming an accompanying band whose membership changed as they tired, fell behind, and were replaced by fresh ones. The masses of cheering spectators thickened as the leading runner neared the stadium.

A cyclist pedaled ahead to counter reports of Flack's impending entry. A scurrying official rushed to the royal box and from there word rushed through the stadium as the first confirming shouts of "Elleen! Elleen!" ("A Greek! A Greek!") were heard from the mobs outside. The Athens chief of police on his huge horse forced a path into the stadium. Pale and covered with dust, but still hammering the road at a steady pace, Spiridon Loues ignited the crowd as he entered the stadium. The little peasant was greeted by the tall Prince Constantine and still taller Prince George, both of whom jogged at his side. They were accompanied by dozens of puffing functionaries who tried to protect the runner from the surging crowds. The officials themselves were waving handkerchiefs as if they were the flags the spectators had. Thousands were weeping openly. All had abandoned themselves to jubilation. During the last few meters the princes were nearly carrying the hero and almost neglected to snap the tape in their eagerness to present the marathon winner to their father. This normally quiet personage had meanwhile torn loose the brim of his gold-embroidered naval cap because of his frantic waving.

Upright and proud, though his uniform could barely be seen, Spiridon Loues watched as the blue and white flag of Greece rose, followed by his number 17, to the top of the flagpole. Bands (which no one heard) played the national anthem. Someone whispered in Spiridon's ear that wealthy ladies were tossing down their jewels. [12] Even the visitors now allowed that it would have been sad to see a foreigner win this race. And then in this supercharged atmosphere, joy was added to joy when the second and third trotters to the finish were also Greeks. Next came Kellner, the Hungarian, and then, incredibly, five more Greeks. Lermusieux actually finished and entered the stadium jabbering and waving his white gloves in attempts to explain what had happened. [13]

Immediately after he won the race on that Friday afternoon, April 10, 1896, Loues became, rather appropriately for a Greek hero, surrounded with a whole cycle, indeed several cycles, of myth. He was twenty-four years old, modest and abstemious, with handsome features and the slender frame of a long-distance runner. But beyond this, there is great confusion about Spiridon Loues. Was he a well-to-do farmer, a very poor peasant, or a soldier? Did he run so resolutely because he wished to please his father or to make an impression on the obdurate parents of a girl he loved? Did he merely sleep soundly the night before the race or did he pray the night through and, before dawn, receive a message from the Virgin who assured him of victory?[14] Did he desperately seek royal clemency for an imprisoned brother? This story was laid to rest when it developed that he had no brother at all, in prison or anywhere else.

Shortly after his race was over, though his countrymen were offering him heaps of drachmas and merchandise, Loues himself could not be found. Word did get out that the hero could accept none of the gifts because he needed his amateur status to win in future Olympic Games. And, of course, such guarantees of nonacceptance only raise the extravagance of offers to the runner. But Spiridon Loues could do nothing to prevent several cafés from changing their names to his, which they did overnight. In fact, the victor was secluded with his family and close friends back in Marousi. Journalists desperate for copy contrived biographical tales that have, since then, made suspect almost every account of his origin and of his preparations for the race. In the heat of the moment, reporters even sought out men said to *resemble* the Olympic hero in order to furnish illustrative copy for the yearning public. Some photos of a handsome fellow in fustanella that were vended in the streets were later proven to be those of a model.

Back in the stadium after the Loues victory, the overwrought crowds for once behaved badly during the last events of the day. The Greeks desperately yearned for more victories. The wrestling matches were dramatically placed on a square, lightly sanded spot in the center of the field in the stadium. Ugly protests rose from large areas of the stands when, in one elimination bout, two famed Greeks, Tsitas and Christopoulos, were matched against each other. The crowd expected that each would wrestle with foreigners and that both would emerge victorious. Then there were disgruntled murmurings when the crowd learned that the fair Mr. Elliot was matched against Karl Schumann, the German turner. Schumann was five feet four inches, crafty and quick. He had entered several events besides the gymnastics, and one observer later declared that, although Schumann was one of the oldest competitors in Athens, he was the best athlete there.[15] Astonishingly, Schumann easily downed Elliot, who was a full foot taller. Darkness fell and in the tavernas that night the Athenian populace cursed their villain as they praised their hero. Early the next morning Schumann also won, with more difficulty, over the Greek champion, Tsitas. The crowd then demanded that the squat German also grapple with Christopoulos, who had earlier lost to Tsitas. Although such a match would be against the rules, Christopoulos was actually sought out, but the candidate confessed that he had been incapacitated in his last fall the day before. After some delay, Schumann and the crowd together watched the rise of the black and white flag of imperial Germany followed by Schumann's number.

Curiously, the sharp boost to Greek pride due to the marathon victory had a corollary effect that the Americans enjoyed. The athletes from the New World became ungrudgingly admired. The college boys easily replaced the Hungarians in the public eye, and their spine-chilling hurrahs produced widespread fascination. The king, once at the stadium and once at a banquet, sent his uniformed aide-de-camp to request repetitions of some especially barbarous cheers. That the boys had incorporated "Zito Hellas!" into their own yells added a further solvent for the already melting Greek hearts. While sightseeing, the Americans were greeted with cries of "Nike! Nike!" ("Victory! Victory!") and storekeepers invited them to help themselves to free merchandise. One haberdasher succeeded, against the sincere protests of the crisp Ivy Leaguers, in forcing them to take three neckties apiece.[16] In the evening packs of students followed the boys and "serenaded" them below their hotel windows with bravely attempted reprises, plus some Hellenized versions, of the Americans' cheers.[17]

One Athenian newspaper accounted for the American's athletic prowess by noting that in their composite blood they "joined the inherited athletic training of the Anglo-Saxon to the wild impetuosity of the redskin."[18] A Greek journalist wrote that Garrett, after his unexpected victory in the shot put, had cabled Princeton, "Gouskos conquered Europe, but I conquered the world!" In the ensuing fuss, the reporter confessed that the message was fictional, but boasted of the news reported, because he felt this was the telegram that Garrett *ought* to have sent. Another observed that the athletes from the United States, just before running or jumping, bowed their heads and said "American prayers."[19]

It was easy for the Greeks to admire the exotics from distant America. The youths were blameless. They were uninfected by the contagious European rivalries which had for decades made political life uncertain in the young and poor nation. A bearded Orthodox priest frequently bent forward to the American spectator in front of him to ask smilingly, "Is that one of yours?" and added after the frequent affirmative responses, "Yours are doing well." Flack, who won all the distance races but the marathon, was denied his distinguishing nationality. One educated Greek, whose notions of geography were nevertheless vague, when told that the great man with the long, stringy legs was Australian, replied, "Australian? Why that is the same thing."[20] An American "tone" in Athens was heightened by the presence of the hundreds of officers and sailors of the cruiser *San Francisco* in the harbor at Piraeus. The navy men were the happy recipients of an overflow of goodwill. On April 11 they held a reception on the ship for the American athletes. The navy band played a concert that started with the "Star-Spangled Banner" and advanced through Waldteuffel, von Suppé, and Sousa waltzes and marches.[21]

On the sixth and seventh days of the Olympic Games, Saturday and Sunday, April 11 and 12, there were a variety of events at several sites in Athens. These events included the wrestling finals, swimming, tennis, and cycling. At the shooting gallery, in the first competition of Saturday, Sumner Paine took the prize in revolvers at thirty meters while second place went to the versatile Jensen, who was earlier the winner in the two—

handed press and a competitor in the rope climb. In the target shooting for pistols at twenty-four meters the first and second places went to two Greeks, Phrangoudhis and Orphanidhis respectively. The shooting competitions were finished a couple of days later with the rifles at three hundred meters. In this event Orphanidhis was first, while Phrangoudhis was second.

On April 11 the weather was clear and sunny, which cheered the impatient swimmers. The organizers had assembled the necessary equipment at the shallow bay of Zéa at Piraeus. The patrician homes surrounding the waterfront were ornamented with bunting and on the shore there was a small, baroque platform for the royal family. Dipping barges and launches, decorated with flags and garlands, held starters, judges, and (in case anyone came to grief) doctors. The sole American competitor had registered for the first event, the one hundred meters (there were no divisions for special strokes, no were there any relays). He was accustomed to the pools at home and did not know that the Mediterranean in early April is icy. At the starter's shot he flung out his length, splendidly splashed, then rose screaming, "Jesu Christo! I'm freezing!" and lashed out for the float he had left so gloriously a moment before. For him the Olympics were over. [22] A Hungarian, Alfred Hoyos, won the race; a Greek, Chorophas, was second. Then there was a special and odd (for the Olympics, at least) 100-meter race for crew members of the royal Greek navy. All were pleased, if not surprised, when the first, second, and subsequent places were taken by Greeks. The official winning time for his race must be given here. It was 2:20.

Three shivering entrants were then taken out of the bay on a little steam launch for the start of the 500-meter race. A pistol-equipped starter was with them and simply guessed as to the proper distance they were to swim to shore. An Austrian, P. Neumann, won, with a Greek second. For the 1,200-meter race the launch went far outside the bay of Zéa. In order to synchronize the swimmers at the start and the stop watches at the finish, a blast from a cannon on shore announced the start. For more than ten minutes the frigid swimmers could not be seen, then one perceived whipping arms and a few bobbing heads—one far ahead of the rest. Hoyos, the Hungarian, finished two minutes before his nearest rival, a Greek. We can note here that of the swimmers, only Hoyos and the delicate American wore bathing suits of thin, clinging material that permitted some freedom of movement.

In the meantime, the spectacle at the velodrome on Saturday, April 11, was less grim than it had been during the 100-kilometer race. The sun was shining. The brass orchestra of the royal navy was placed in the center of the ring to supply airs and patriotic marches. The royal family was on hand to inspire Greek contestants. The scheduled races were over distances of ten kilometers, two kilometers, and a sprint of one lap around the track which had a circumference of 333⅓ meters. The victor in all these events was a nose-on-the-front-wheel-bottom-in-the-air Frenchman, Emile Masson. In each race Greeks followed him closely to the finish. On each of the next two days there were popular cycling events. The more sensational in terms of its drawing power was a specially contrived cycling "marathon" of eighty-seven kilometers. The course went from the velodrome to Marathon and returned to the velodrome in Athens. By this time, anything called "marathon" was bound to electrify the whole nation. The road itself was rutted and had been difficult enough for the nimble foot racers. Despite the glamour of this "marathon" there were just six starters. Two were foreigners: Goedrich, another of the stern, versatile Germans, and Battel, a servant at the British embassy whom several other Englishmen had tried to bar from entering the race since he was not a gentleman and therefore was not in their eyes an amateur. The road out of Athens was again lined with optimistic spectators in numbers out of all proportion to the quality of the cyclists and the organizers' preparations for such an event.

Goedrich tried the technique of Loues and jolted along at a steady pace far behind his more eager opponents. Constantinidhis, the Greek favorite, was ahead at the switch-back at Marathon, but on his return his cycle faltered and collapsed. Before he had adjusted the spare provided by one of his pacers, Battel rolled by and into the lead. Then, just outside Athens the English youth, jarred and near exhaustion, fell and scraped himself badly. A little after passing Battel, who was attempting to repair himself and his machine, Constantinidhis also spilled, totally wrecked his second cycle, and badly sprained his arm. Undaunted, he snatched the bike of an observer and was the first to reach the velodrome, whereupon he touched off another installment of mass hysteria in Athens. The outsmarted, plodding German came in second, twenty minutes later. Battel, shaken and smeared with grime and dried blood, was the only other finisher.

The last of the long cycling events occurred a day later. This was a twelve-hours race that began under the stars at the velodrome at five o'clock in the morning of April 13, with six chilly entries and almost no one to cheer them on. Maximum distances traveled would determine the winner. At noon, seven hours later, there were just three spinning cyclists. At two o'clock the judges had to count the laps only of Kiping, the other English servant, and of an Austrian, Schmall. By now, because of the pitiable condition of the surviving pair, this race was a spectacle for the strong of stomach. Neither man had eaten and had only sips of liquid. Both were squalid from excreta and delirious from fatigue. Their churning legs had swollen gruesomely. Kiping's arms were swollen too, but still he battled on. Both could be heard audibly weeping as they passed and were passed in turn. Schmall was the winner with nine hundred revolutions—about three hundred kilometers. His rival finished just 333⅓ meters (one lap) behind.

Several other events were also finished up in these last few days. An Englishman named Boland, who had happened to be in Athens as a tourist, won the singles in tennis and shared victory in the doubles with Traun, one of the Germans. Greeks took second place in both events.

We should note here that ever since the Games had begun, officials and sportsmen (at the behest of Coubertin) had been attempting to begin a series of yachting events. As in other events, there were disputes over the rules and over the small number of entries, but these problems had not stopped the planning, both in Greece and abroad, for the sailing competitions. The contests were dropped because of the inclement weather, as wind storms had occasionally reached gale force.

Other parts of the program that never materialized were the competitions in music. No foreign entries appeared and various Greek orchestras and bands that had expressed interest later claimed they had lacked time to practice. Since few of the musicians were first–rate anyway, most officials were relieved when this part of the schedule was abandoned. One cultural embellishment of the festival consisted of a series of unusual performances of Sophocles' *Antigone*. A Mr. Sakellarides had composed special music, based upon Byzantine models, for the choruses of the play. A musical claque, opposed to the composer, prepared to cause a hubbub at the first performance, but was agreeably astonished at the debut and caused no disturbances at subsequent successes when the classic play was performed once more in Athens and once at Piraeus during the festival.[23] The addition of music and drama to the program at Athens was claimed to be a harking back to the inclusion of nonathletic events in the ancient Olympic Games.

Although not classed as competitions, other spectacles were featured at the international sports festival. On the first night, for example, the city was illuminated by all the newly installed gas and electric street lights. On the second evening the Acropolis was the site of special firework displays which lit the majestic columns of the Parthenon and other temples with shifting hues of yellow, green, and red. Citizens were kept off the boulevards by the weather on the third and fourth evenings, but the "marathon evening" was clear. On that evening the general euphoria served to heighten the magic (as well as to mask the incongruity) of a "Venetian" evening at the harbor of Piraeus. Gaslight was joined by hanging strings of Chinese lanterns containing candles, and there were flares from the ships in the port. The *San Francisco* outclassed all the other ships. The entire shape of the heavy cruiser as well as its lines of rigging were marked by strings of electric bulbs. An enormous American shield in red, white, and blue lights blazed at the bow. The spectacle required two thousand light bulbs and all the current from the whining dynamos of the warship. On this "Venetian" evening, fraternal, social, educational, and professional groups of the city marched in torchlight processions before the royal family, who had placed themselves on a balcony at the Piraeus city hall. The city choir performed a cantata, "The Young Sailor," and the municipal orchestra played sections from "Lohengrin" in the public park. Very late, rockets, shooting stars, and Roman candles were touched off from a raft in the harbor.

Athens was larger than Piraeus and could hold grander spectacles. Sunday, April 12, was the day of Constantinidhis's triumph in the cycling marathon. At dusk that day paraders assembled on Athena Street, one of the longest and widest in the city. Then at nine o'clock began the most ambitious of the Olympic extravaganzas. A troop of cavalry in jangling parade hardware and high plumes led the procession around Constitution Square and before the palace where the monarchs and their children once more placed themselves at the foci of admiration. Next in the procession came local bands, marching provincial musicians, and some three hundred caretakers of the stadium carrying banners of the competing nations. Then there were army regiments, crews from warships, and two thousand students from the Athenian lycées and the university. Marchers with free hands carried paper Chinese lanterns with candles inside or held flaming torches. Once assembled, the paraders could not be contained by the square, but spilled over into the streets in all directions singing the Greek national anthem. The happy patriots would not disperse until long after midnight.

Another ceremonial event was the king's "breakfast" on Sunday, April 12. Really another banquet, this party was held in the colonnaded ballroom of the royal palace. The invitations requested the three hundred guests—athletes, journalists, and officials—to appear in ordinary street dress. Only the Hungarians showed up en masse in black evening wear. The camaraderie at the breakfast caused it to be long remembered. Most remarkable and much commented upon was the intense pleasure of the king as he doted on Spiridon Loues, who was present with his father. The king was in the glittering uniform of an admiral; the peasant was in the narrow jacket, flaring skirt, and tights of fustanella. This was the menu for the breakfast:

Tranches de Poisson frit, à la Colbert
Pommes de Terre
Pilaff à Volaille
Filet de Boeuf rôté
Purée d'Epinards
Jambon et Dinde froide à la Gelée
Salade à la Russe
Crême glacée à l'Ananas
Achaïa, Vin blanc Château de Décelie, Château Larose
Cesarewitch, Malvoisie[24]

Not a very elaborate meal according to the banqueting standards of the time, but it was suitably international and was, after all, only a breakfast. Even on this Sunday morning there were customary toasts, some of the best of which were offered by the usually quiet but now aroused and loquacious monarch. His last toast had a peculiar paragraph in it that evoked great enthusiasm and cheers from all but a very few guests, one of whom, Pierre de Coubertin, was particularly astonished, piqued, and alerted. The king said:

Greece, the mother and nurse of the Olympic Games in antiquity, has labored to celebrate the Games once more before the eyes of Europe and the new world. Since the success of the Games has passed all expectations, we hope that our guests, who have honored us with their presence, will select Athens as the peaceful meeting place of all nations, as the stable and permanent seat of the Olympic Games.[25]

The response of Philemon, the chief executive of the Games in Athens, was suitably adulatory:

The diamonds that have fallen from your mouth, oh Sire, shine so brilliantly that our most strenuous eloquence is made to appear pale. Perhaps our enthusiasm and sincerity can. . . .[26]

The athletes went to many parties. The mayor of Athens gave a banquet in the shaded village of Cephissa at the foot of Mt. Pentilicous. Demitrios Bikelas offered a special banquet for the foreign athletes. Madame Schliemann, the proud widow of the great archaeologist who had excavated Troy and Mycenae, had a reception at her country villa in the vale of Daphne. While there, talk between the American youths and the royal princes became bogged in confusion over the meaning of such phrases as "bases," "innings," and "strikes" connected with the American national game. In the ensuing demonstration—aided, with characteristic Yankee ingenuity, by a walking stick and a handy piece of fruit—there were moments of acute embarrassment when Prince George's court uniform was speckled by particles of a splattered orange.[27]

The final day of the Games (several times put off because of bad weather) was April 15, a sunny Wednesday, and was devoted to the conferring of prizes. Ticket holders were admitted to the stadium first, but after the arrival of the royal ᶜ the people outside (some of whom had been waiting since the early morning) were freely admitted to fill every spot in the stands. More crowds covered the hills nearby. The king stood on a raised platform before a long table that held the awards. Before the ceremonies began he was addressed by an Oxford student, G. S. Robertson, with a "Pindaric" ode in classical Greek which Robertson had composed for the occasion. A Captain Hadjipetros was the herald who summoned the individual winners, all of whom had assembled on the field before the officials. Each athlete, as he was called, walked up a few steps, accepted his trophy with mumbled thanks and returned to the select group of visitors. First place winners received a fresh olive branch from the ancient altis at Olympia, an engraved certificate (the Americans called them "diplomas"), and a silver medal. The second place winners accepted a laurel branch, a certificate, and a bronze medal. Robertson, the English Olympic laureate, also received, appropriately, a laurel branch.

There were, in addition, certain extra awards. Gravellote, the outstanding French fencer, accepted a silver cup. One Greek marksman received a richly hand-tooled rifle; another, a pistol. Garrett, besides his several branches, certificates, and medals, also took home the very discus he had heaved in that last victorious throw, a silver vase from Crown Princess Sophie, and a marble bust of the goddess Athena executed by the same sculptor who had rendered the monumental likeness of Averoff. The congratulatory recognition that greeted the rangy American was tinged with some regrets, for these last items were intended never to leave Greece. Then the crowd received a treat, as the Greek triumph in the marathon was officially rewarded. Loues, who had rather avoided the public eye to this point, came forward with slow steps in dazzling white fustanella to receive, besides the usual prizes, a lovely antique amphora that had been awarded to a victorious athlete in Athens more than two thousand years before. He also accepted the special, heavy silver urn that the Parisian, Michel Bréal, had contributed to establish the supreme distance race. As the hero of heroes mounted the king's platform, packed thousands exploded into volleys of mad cheers and frantically waved their handkerchiefs and little national pennants. A director of the revels had arranged for the release of hundreds of white pigeons who trailed ribbons of the national colors while, as scheduled, some spectators tossed flower petals into the air.

Then the champions proceeded around the track proudly clasping their olive and laurel branches. They were arranged by nationality and were followed by bands playing several national anthems. Modest and upright, Loues led the parade while steadily waving a miniature Greek flag that an adoring country-man had thrust into his hand. After the tumult that accom-panied their circuit the group assembled once more before the king, who announced, "I proclaim the ending of the first Olympic Games."

7

AFTER THE GAMES

WITH HIS LAST toast at the Sunday breakfast for the visiting athletes, we recall, King George had announced his hope "that our guests, who have honored us with their presence, will select Athens as the peaceful meeting place of all nations, as the stable and permanent seat of the Olympic Games."[1] We also recall that, from the very beginning of his planning to have international sports festivals, Pierre de Coubertin had envisioned them as regular but "ambulatory," and that the first such international meeting was originally planned for the Paris Exposition of 1900. In Coubertin's mind, the offering of the first meeting of the modern Olympic Games to Athens in 1896 was a most exceptional favor. Thus Coubertin, who was present at that breakfast, felt that if the Greeks were to keep the Olympic Games it would be equivalent of "the suicide of my efforts."[2]

Now it appeared, particularly to the Greeks, that there were good reasons to hold the subsequent Olympic festivals in Athens. Despite dozens of petty irritations—the misunderstandings of international rules by Greek judges, the disputed awarding of places in a race that appeared to some to be a dead heat, the condition of the track at the stadium, the high prices for seats at the athletic events, the point system in the gymnastic events, and many others—the whole pageant had been rather well run. All visitors commented on the keen pleasure the Greeks had taken in being hosts for this festival. In contrast to the dismal state of the Greek government's finances at the same time, there had been plenty of money for organization and festivities. Many Greeks, particularly those in important places, believed that their triumph would be a decisive step toward improving their prestige in the world. The fact that there had been few foreigners in Athens, and that there were almost no foreigners of political significance to enjoy in person or even hear about the revived Olympic Games, was blithely passed over. [3]

Much of the explanation for the origin and continued survival of the modern Greek nation can be traced to the profound philhellenism of the ruling classes of western Europe. The success of the revolts of the 1820s would have been inconceivable without diplomatic and other pressure from the Great Powers against the Ottoman Empire. During the rest of the nineteenth century the young nation depended upon European investment and European diplomacy in order to maintain the independence and to assure the survival of the people who, as they themselves ceaselessly reiterated, were the heirs of the greatest culture the world had ever known. It was only to be expected that the modern Greeks would plan to inspire more of the philhellenism that had revived their own spirits and advertised Greek culture to the world.

The ruling dynasty, particularly, had reason to want the establishment of a whole series of Athenian "Olympic Games." The family of George I had close blood ties with the ruling houses of England, Germany, and Russia. In the minds of some Greeks, these connections were essential to maintain the prestige and independence of a poor nation bordered by enemies. Well-staged Olympic Games would force upon the monarchs of the greater and lesser powers the periodic recognition of the imperative to preserve and foster the birthplace of western culture. But there was an additional reason for the king and the crown prince to promote the idea of periodic international festivals in their capital. The financial crisis which had worsened in 1894 had limited the functioning of the bureaucracy, which in turn was dependent upon the parliament, which itself had very low prestige. Therefore many of the happy results of the Games in the capital were attributed to the royal family, whose constitutional power was severely limited but whose members had been so devoted to ceremonial appearances during the Games.

The campaign of the Greeks against ambulatory Olympic Games was even given a boost by the American athletes who, warmed by the manifest affection of the natives, signed a petition in favor of keeping the Olympic Games where the Greeks felt they belonged—in Greece. With good reason, therefore, many Greeks began planning for repeat performances in 1900, 1904, and so on.

One might apportion some of the blame for a subsequent political disaster for the Greeks on their distorted view of their strengths. Elated by their success in pageantry (if not their athletic prowess) at the Olympic Games, they may well have overestimated their military and diplomatic strengths as well.

The desire on the part of the Greeks all over the Mediterranean to unite in one political union had a long history. The political fate of Greeks under Turkish rule in Crete had become a very serious emotional issue in the course of 1896 and then, shortly after the Olympic Games, exploded. On February 5, 1897, the Greek Consul in Crete sent a telegram to Athens stating that the Turks were about to massacre the Greeks on the island. Turks had massacred Greeks before and the Greeks had skirmished with the Turks before, but the claim of the consul this time had little basis in fact. Nevertheless, all Athens became inflamed with patriotic, irridentist indignation. Even if it had wished to do so, the government, whose premier was still the demagogic Theodoros Deligiannes, could scarcely resist the pressure to punish the Cretan Muslims and effect *enosis*, or political union, with the mainland. Some responsible Greeks (including Diligiannes himself) held back, for they realized that

effective military preparations were nonexistent and nonar-
rangeable. Then, in a fit of opportunism, the royal family
attempted to ride *this* wave to popularity. Princes Constantine
and George actually led armies against the Turks in Thessaly.

The campaigns were calamities. Riccotti Garibaldi, son of
Giuseppe and, like his father, a crusader for the rights of
oppressed peoples, joined the Greeks. Along with many other
Italian volunteers, he was disgusted by what he saw. Greece
itself was in danger of being overrun by the better-armed,
better-led Turks. The inability of the Great Powers to make
quick decisions only intensified the disaster. Once more
Deligiannes resigned the premiership. Eventually the powers
intervened diplomatically, this time not only to save Greek
territorial integrity, but to save the dynasty, which by a characteristically vaulting diversion of aroused public sentiment was
being blamed for the disasters. An armistice was signed on May
20, 1897, and a peace treaty on December 4, 1897.[4]

Then began an especially dismal period in Greek history.
The wisest Hellenic statesman of the age, Spiridon Tricoupis—
who, we remember, was Coubertin's opponent over the issue of
staging the Athens Games in the first place—had died on
April 11, 1896. He was in exile in Cannes in southern France
and was therefore spared the knowledge that the Olympic
Games he had opposed were triumphant. An international
control commission was put in charge of the Greek fiscal
system. Through the next ten years there was continued irre-
sponsibility and bitterness in political life. It is possible that
the erratic constitutional meddling of the ambitious Constantine
(who ruled as king from 1913 to 1917 and again from 1920 to
1922) may be dated back, and attributed, to the surge of self-
confidence and popularity he felt during his appearances and
performances at the Olympic Games of 1896.[5]

During the Games in Athens, the more realistic Greek
planners were much more interested in the likely political
benefits of the festival than they were in noteworthy athletic

performances or the effects the festival might have on the physical health of the nation. The usual reasons given for staging athletic festivals—to give the public an opportunity to appreciate high performance, for example—were peculiar to the Anglo-Saxon mentality. The staging of their own particular kind of athletic festivals in order to inspire more broadly based physical education was an established element only in the countries of northern and central Europe, particularly Germany. The fact that there were so many native entries in the Athens Games is more attributable to temporary enthusiasm than to any developed athletic spirit.

After the Games were over, the pledged financial help of George Averoff permitted the Greeks to continue to restore the stadium of Herodes Atticus. The trellised tribunes at the various other sporting sites were maintained for their anticipated use in the next Olympic Games in Athens. Amid a series of grim economic and political humiliations, particularly the military defeat of 1897, the Greeks recalled their international festivals as an oasis of happiness.

A vivid reminder of this happiness was Spiridon Loucs. He ran demonstration "marathons" and modestly accepted the adulation of his countrymen, but he never again competed in an international meet. Loues did, however, make one stunningly impressive public appearance at the Olympic Games forty years after his first triumph. During the opening ceremonies of the Olympic Games in Berlin in August, 1936, he stepped forward from the Greek team on the infield at the great stadium. He was a little stooped and had a brown face that was wrinkled like a prune. He was dressed in the tight black vest and white skirt of fustenella, and was smiling warmly as he presented Adolf Hitler with a branch of olive, symbolizing peace, from the sacred grove at Olympia.

Loues's time for his marathon victory, 2:58:50, is one of the few records set in Athens that looks almost respectable by present-day standards. The record was not broken until the

1908 Olympics in London and then only by two seconds. However, a closer examination of the changing length of the marathon race is necessary here. Loues ran twenty-four miles, 1,500 yards, a little less than twenty-five miles. The modern distance for the marathon, as run in 1908 and made official in 1924, is twenty-six miles, 385 yards. Therefore, despite the extraordinary notoriety of Loues's performance, it was more or less in keeping with the rest of the best athletic performances recorded in Athens in 1896.

We ought not, however, judge the performances of the athletes of 1896 by the standards of today. There are several reasons for this. The abstraction of high performance into "records" was something that had entered the minds of only a very few American and British athletes and their fans. The very notion of a track record was itself little more than three decades old.[6] And the upper-crust American and English athletes in Athens were, by the standard of the sports world of the later twentieth century, dilettantes. Most of the English were there by accident, and the Americans were there to have a good time. Amateur sportsmen in the 1890s were drawn from a tiny, pampered minority. Today the world's billions are canvassed for the potential to set new sports records.

We can, however, note several factors that may help to justify the reputations of the athletic heroes of 1896. As noted earlier, the Greek runner in ancient times not only had to sprint, he also had to negotiate about-face turns. Although the track at the stadium of Herodes Atticus had been widened by setting the first rows of the seats back, the curves were still sharp and required significant reductions in speed. The track surface was loose. The ash or hickory pole used by the vaulters was heavy and rigid. The "western roll" had not been invented yet, so the high jumpers went over with a scissors kick. The fastest hurdlers still went over the barriers knee first with the foot of the forward leg bent back. The straight-legged *grand jete*, which was much faster, was first observed by an international audience in Paris in 1900. We recall that Robert Garrett was the victor in the then-novel discus event and that he had practiced just one day for his record of 29.15 meters (95' 7¾"). In September, 1896, Garrett wrote:

I do not think a fairly strong man with a long [sic] arm should have much difficulty in throwing this [discus] 120 or 130 feet after earnest practice. I have myself thrown it about 102 feet in practice in May last, although I fear I could not do that in competition.[7]

Sure enough, the record for the discus throw was pegged at almost 129 feet at the 1904 Olympics. The record is now over two hundred feet.

Here are some more of the "records" of 1896. The winning times for the track events were: 100 meters, 12 seconds; 400 meters, 54.2 seconds; 800 meters, 2 minutes 11 seconds; 1,500 meters, 4 minutes 33.2 seconds; 110–meter hurdles, 17.6 seconds. Marks for the field events were: running broad jump, 20 feet 9¾ inches; running high jump, 5 feet 11¼ inches; triple jump, 45 feet; pole vault, 10 feet 9¾ inches; shot put, 36 feet 2 inches. Laurenceton Elliot lifted with one arm a dumbbell weighing 156 pounds 8 ounces. Viggo Jensen, the Dane, pressed 245 pounds 12 ounces. The distances and times for the swimming events were: 100 meters, 1 minute 22.2 seconds; 500 meters, 8 minutes 12.6 seconds; 1,200 meters, 18 minutes 22.2 seconds. The best cycling times were: 2 kilometers, 4 minutes 56 seconds; 10 kilometers, 17 minutes 54.2 seconds; 100 kilometers, 3 hours 8 minutes 19 seconds. Most of these performances could now be surpassed by good high school athletes.

Few of the foreign athletes in Athens were of championship caliber even by the American, English, or German standards of the time. The German athletes were rounded up at the last minute. Though they were good and versatile, their circles of competition at home had not become obsessed with performance for its own sake and the setting of records. The Olympic tennis champion, I. P. Boland, just happened to be in Athens and purchased his racket on the spot in order to compete. The hurdler Grantley Goulding and the Australian distance runner Edwin Flack were known in England as exceptional performers, but did not make their expected marks in Athens. Some of the team from the Boston Athletic Association, however, were of world championship caliber. Thomas Burke, James Connolly, Thomas Curtis, and Ellery Clark—all from the B.A.A.—were tops or nearly so in the United States. Yet none of them in Athens equaled his best performances at home. All the Americans were in less than perfect shape when they arrived in Athens. And once they were on the scene the competitions began almost at once, as did the distractions. The Yanks treated the whole show rather as a lark. It was impossible to duplicate the high tension for performance of the intercollegiate rivalries of the Ivy League.

The American public has always been especially fond of winners. News of the accomplishments in Athens of the Princeton and Harvard men on the American Olympic team found its way back to the States and was reported not only in the New York and Boston papers but in many newspapers in the American midwest.[8] The four juniors from Princeton found time to visit Pompeii as they waited in Naples for their ship, but had to rush back to finish their semester and to compete in meets with Yale and Columbia. A crowd of one thousand greeted them at the station in Princeton when they arrived. The Olympic heroes were then carried to the campus on the shoulders of their cheering admirers. The town's bells rang and there was a grand bonfire to celebrate their triumphs. All their trophies were admired, especially Robert Garrett's discus, which was described by a sports writer as being "like a flap-jack, but thick in the center."[9]

Ellery Clark was the only man from Boston who had to get back to Harvard. Connolly had quit and the rest had graduated. So the Bostonians visited Rome and Paris on their way to

Bremen to sail on the *Lahn* as their adventures were being
reported and embellished at home. In New York on May 7,
1896, a band on the dock in Hoboken greeted them with "See,
the Conquering Hero Comes." The boys were at once swept off
to a banquet at the Knickerbocker Club in Manhattan. In
describing his stay in Athens to a reporter, Thomas Burke said,

> The Greeks were not in it with our team. Those fellows are
> undoubtedly great athletes, but they don't know the game. They run
> like chumps. They are not up to snuff and know few of the
> ropes.
> They took their defeat very cheerfully. . . . The Greeks, from the
> highest to the lowest, treated us with great consideration, and did
> everything possible to show their appreciation of our presence in their
> country. [10]

When their train was greeted in Boston some of the boys were
wearing red fezzes. They had incorporated "Zito Hellas!" into
their cheers and explained to clusters of reporters that it meant
"Hurrah for Athens!" Blake was especially closely questioned
by reporters about the race from Marathon to Athens which he
called "the 23-mile straightaway." Boston politicians attempted
to outshine one another in the grandiloquence of their praise for
these fine Bostonians and patriotic Americans. There was an
official reception in Faneuil Hall where any Bostonian who
wished could shake the athletes' hands. The largest banquet for
the boys was at the Vendome Hotel and was attended by 250
persons. [11]

So, in a small way, the ideas of modern "Olympic Games"
and of festive international expositions of sport were introduced
to the American reading public. The discus throw—or, as it was
then called, the discus "put"—began to appear as an event on
the program of university track and field meets. Garrett, the
authority on the subject, cautioned American coaches to scorn a
seven-pound discus that was sometimes used and to use the
heavier, four-kilogram international one. Very long distance

races of ten or even more miles were not unknown in the Northeast before the athletes of the Boston Athletic Association returned from Greece, but several American runners now began to train for still longer races. The B.A.A. held its first marathon in April of 1897. The winner was J. J. McDermott who covered the distance of twenty-five miles in 2 hours 55 minutes 10 seconds, which beat Spiridon Loues's time over a shorter distance. Soon one heard of marathons being held in other places in the United States and Canada.[12]

The events in Athens were scarcely noticed in the British press. There had been only scattered and scornful remarks on the preparations before the games began. The few British athletes on hand appeared only as individuals. There was no club participation. There was but one article in a British magazine which reported the Athens Games.[13] Much of the disdain can probably be traced to the exclusiveness of British amateur sport. "Clean" sport, according to the traditional upper-class English view, would be allowed to exist in its pure form only twice: for a while the ancient Greeks possessed it, and now it dwelt exclusively among the Anglo-Saxons (particularly those with independent incomes). Thus it was idle to notice so-called sporting events staged by swarthy, excitable Levantines who happened to inhabit a historic and lovely landscape.

In Germany, Austria, and Hungary, the events of the first modern Olympic Games were remarked upon only in a few of the turners' newsletters. Willibald Gebhardt and a few others continued to favor the participation of Germans in international sports festivals on the terms established by foreigners. Germans appeared and won medals in the Olympic Games of 1900, 1904, and 1908.[14] Gebhardt was eventually successful as a candidate for membership in Coubertin's International Olympic Committee. But in German physical education circles the great struggle between turning and sport (and their respective ideologies) had just begun and was to affect German turning, German sport, and the Olympic movement later into the twentieth century.

The French cyclists and fencers who had been victorious were celebrities only within their individual clubs. The time was still far off when Frenchmen could fashion heroes out of those who were amateur sports champions. The authoritative source of news on what happened in Athens was Coubertin himself. Significantly, Coubertin's most detailed reportage of the festivities in Athens was never prominently published in French, but appeared in the prestigious American magazine the *Century* in November, 1896.[15] As is characteristic of almost all of Coubertin's writing for publication in these early years of his work for international sport, Coubertin revealed none of his personal bitterness. He did not mention that his own role had been decisive and that he had been pushed aside by the Greeks, but instead gave a picture of a healthy, burgeoning Olympic movement. He, of course, had good reasons for discussing the movement rather than the well-staged events in Athens, because he opposed the plans of the Greeks to prevent the new Olympics from being ambulatory, that is, under Coubertin's control.

When Coubertin returned to Paris from Athens, he began at once to prepare for what was originally to have been the first modern Olympic Games. As was noted earlier, Coubertin had previously arranged a conference on physical education that was officially included in the huge Universal Exposition of 1889 in Paris. At the time, Coubertin had suggested to some directors of that exposition that the wider embrace of the next exposition might include some sections on sport and athleticism. The Third Republic published a degree on July 13, 1892, that the next Universal International Exposition in Paris would be held from April 15 through October 15, 1900. It was announced (in a claim that was characteristic of the optimistic century just ending) that the next exposition would have historical exhibits showing the progress of mankind. The planning of the exposition would be rigidly centralized under one civil servant, Alfred Picard, the Commissioner General.

Before Coubertin had even considered the possibility of holding the Olympic Games in Athens, he and a philhellene professor and gymnast, Georges Strehly, submitted a detailed proposal for athletics at the Exposition of 1900:

The project planned for the erection of a reconstruction of the altis of Olympia within the grounds of the Exposition. In the interior of the monument we would assemble and display objects and documents dealing with sports in antiquity, in the middle ages and in modern times. [16]

Picard, whom Coubertin later called a "dictator," received the project graciously.

After his return from Athens in the summer 1896, Coubertin's energies were devoted to the planning of a yet better meeting of the modern Olympians in Paris in 1900. The stationery of his Comité international olympique had long carried at its head, besides the name of the secretary (himself) and the intimidating list of honorary members, the legend, "Athens 1896, Paris 1900." Picard had in the meantime, without telling Coubertin, entrusted the planning for an exhibition of physical education and sport to a group of bureaucrats in the Ministry of Education over whom the aristocrat had little influence and less control. [17] Coubertin learned upon the publication of an official program, for example, that ice skating had been included in cutlery, sailing among lifesaving, societies of sport in social welfare.

It became clear to Coubertin that he could accomplish none of his objectives by working through the Commissioner General and his subordinate civil servants. Desperate to make concrete his vision, he even tried for a while to find a way to stage the second Olympic Games within Paris but apart from the great exposition, which by the year 1897 had Paris in a turmoil of special construction. These massive preparations, in turn, fed

French expectations of a prestigious international triumph. Significantly, as secretary of the I.O.C., Coubertin had his committee meet in the city of Le Havre in 1897. He later claimed that he wished to have the meeting in Normandy, because it was close to the countryside where he had been so happy as a child and because it was close to the sporting atmosphere of Britain, home of the great Thomas Arnold.[18] There can be little doubt, however, that Coubertin did not want his contacts from abroad to see the preparations in Paris from which he and his projects were being excluded.[19] In fact, Coubertin accomplished little in Le Havre except to reaffirm the existence of the International Olympic Committee and to pass some resolutions favoring Coubertin's conceptions of amateurism. The Olympic Games scarcely entered the discussions.

Nevertheless, the focus of Coubertin's attentions remained in Paris where he continued to seek support and financing for an independent staging of the second Olympic Games in 1900. The institutional instrument to support his claim to be the only leader of athleticism in France was his Union des sociétés françaises des sports athlétiques. He claimed all the members of the constituent societies of the U.S.F.S.A. as members of his "Union." He hoped that the public at large would consider him the only legitimate representative in France of French and even international athletics.

In the meantime, the planning staffs for the exposition, in their eagerness to stage the ultimate world's fair, revealed that the athletic festival they had in mind would include ballooning, billiards, fishing, and even checkers, as well as every other sport one could possibly think of. Track and field events were to be included in Section I of a ten-part "International Congress of Physical Education" that would also include pelote, the Basque game, which would have its own presidents, juries, and awards. The sporting events would be open to all and would take place in many parts of Paris throughout the summer. To Coubertin it all seemed vulgar and chaotic. He had envisaged games for an elite: an elite of contestants, few in number, but consisting of the champion athletes of the world; an elite of spectators, sophisticated people, diplomats, professors, generals, members of the institutes and academies. For all these people, what could be more refined, more ravishing than a garden party at Dampierre, an evening festival on the rue de Varennes, excursions to Esclimont or Bonnelles?[20]

He succeeded in getting some forty Parisians, mostly titled aristocrats, who issued public statements that they were in favor of having the second Olympic Games held outside the exposition. During the year 1898 they met in the Paris hotel of the Vicomte de Rochefoucauld. For the Games of 1900 they favored dropping marksmanship with firearms and adding events for bowmen. Polo and golf were to be added, as was a prize for the most "remarkable" ascent of a mountain since the year 1896. Coubertin claimed strong support from Belgium, Russia, and even Australia. The press of the right was pleased with his progress; some leftists denounced Coubertin's "meetings of counts and marquises."[21]

Commissioner General Picard and his lieutenants (who, Coubertin claimed, knew nothing about sport) ignored Coubertin's propaganda, as did the commissioners general of the nations that would participate in the exposition. Professor William Milligan Sloane of Princeton eventually advised that it would be best to demur. Some counts and marquises felt uneasy at playing rebels and left Coubertin. Finally, early in 1899, Coubertin met with Daniel Mérillon, "Director General of the Athletic Competitions of the Universal Exposition of 1900 in Paris," and agreed to call these competitions the "second Olympic Games."[22]

Then, with characteristic energy and devotion, he decided to make the Games a festive success. During the exposition he gave parties for the international bureaucrats of physical education. However, it appears he spent little time at the many dozens of contests themselves.[23] Few of the vast numbers of tourists in Paris that summer (the events dragged out from the beginning of July through October) knew that Olympic Games were taking place. Many athletes learned that they had participated in the second Olympic Games of the modern era only when they noted the inscriptions to the effect on some of their medals and certificates. Coubertin was inwardly depressed at the reception accorded his selfless energies. His experiences

proved that, in any case, one must make sure that these Games are never again allowed to be annexed to one of these grand fairs in the middle of which their philosophical value evaporates and their educational value is ineffective.[24]

The actual sporting competitions of the exposition, which in the traditional histories of the Olympic movement are called "the second Olympic Games," were naturally full of incident. The number of participants was large, the number of ancestors small. Apart from Coubertin's organizational efforts, there were international meetings of physical educationalists. About all we can attribute to the Paris Games was that they reinforced Coubertin's notions of a four-year periodicity and the principle that the Games should be ambulatory. Some of the events, particularly those of the American track and field athletes, have been sketched in most surveys of the modern Olympic Games.

For years Coubertin and Sloane had assumed that the Olympic Games of 1904 would take place in America, most likely in New York. Chicago was the second choice. But neither gentleman could fabricate an organizational framework or drum up enthusiasm in these cities, and Coubertin went through several years of anguished correspondence and bitter humiliation before he permitted the third Olympic Games to take place in St. Louis in 1904, where they would be subsumed in the great world's fair planned for that city. And Coubertin knew that they would be staged by people far more familiar with carnivals than with his high-toned sports theater. Among a large variety of more or less accepted sports events, there were to be special contests in St. Louis for the world's aborigines. It was also rumored that there were to be "Olympic competitions in tobacco juice spitting. Naturally, Baron Pierre de Coubertin did not bother to appear.

In the meantime, so deep had been the humiliation after the Turkish war of 1897 that the Greek government had not been able to present their own Olympic Games in 1900 and 1904. The Greeks did stage what might be called "rump" Olympic Games in 1906. Here again Coubertin was unrecognized, though the standard of festivity, the breadth of international participation and the performance levels were, as a whole, superior to the Olympic Games of 1896, 1900, 1904, and 1908.

Again in 1908, Coubertin, in order to maintain his principle of four-year periodicity, had been forced to subordinate the Olympic Games to a larger festival, the Franco-British Exposition of 1908. These Olympic Games were especially marked by the disruptive rivalries between the large and patriotically motivated American and British teams.

There were plans to have the festival in Athens take place every four years after 1906 and then establish a regularity in sports festivals like that of ancient times when the Pythian Games took place in those even-numbered years when there was no major festival at Olympia. But the Greeks were never again able to have rump Olympics in Athens.

Through all these years the taste for sports, and its respectability, continued to grow. In the Anglo-Saxon countries many kinds of professional and amateur sport became more widely practiced and viewed—and consequently more deeply institutionalized. Physical education programs became integrated into the systems of public education that were becoming ever more broadly based in Europe and elsewhere. As sports rules were made uniform by international meetings of coaches and trainers, international meets subsequently became much more common. Sports pages appeared in almost all daily newspapers. There were even a few international journals for sport and physical education. Coubertin himself began regularly publishing his *Bulletin du comité international olympique* just after the exposition of 1900 in Paris.

Though the Olympic Games of 1900 and 1904 were polyglot circuses, and the London Games of 1908 were more a contribution to international acrimony than to harmony, Coubertin's public optimism endured. The list of honorary members for the I.O.C. grew ever more distinguished. He added to his letterhead a new symbol of the Olympic movement—the emblem of five rings, each of them a primary color used in the flags of the nations that would compete in the Olympic Games when they were presented as they should be.

Finally, twenty years after Coubertin's public suggestion that the Olympic Games be revived, the Olympics were staged somewhat in accordance with Coubertin's concepts. Colonel Victor Balck, a loyal associate, had arranged for the Olympic Games of 1912 to take place in Stockholm. As in Athens, there was plenty of money, which this time had been raised by a special lottery. The royal family inserted themselves into most of the ceremonies. The Olympic Games in Stockholm were independent of any other distracting public festival and took place in facilities especially designed and built for the occasion. It should also be mentioned here that these were the first Olympics in the course of which athletes other than Americans established many new records.

After the 1912 Games, Coubertin was generally recognized as being the reviver of the modern Olympic Games which now merited a great deal of attention in the newspapers all over the world including even Germany and Japan. The International Olympic Committee was beginning to meet and to discuss rather than waiting to be informed of Coubertin's negotiations by means of his *Bulletin*. Coubertin himself, though he always considered that his work for international sporting festivals was only part of his educational mission, came to the conclusion that fame, such as would fall to him, would be due to the

Olympic Games. After about 1908, his patriotism weakened due to the lack of recognition of it. Appreciation for his labors and his selflessness was always greater outside France than it had been in his native land.

He consented to the awarding of the sixth Olympic Games to the capital city of the German Empire. The Games would take place in 1916. Preparations for a sports festival far more lavish than the one in Stockholm were underway in Berlin when the World War broke out, forcing the sixth Olympic Games to be canceled. In 1918 Coubertin himself left France to spend the rest of his life in Switzerland. From there he was able to maintain the Olympic periodicity by awarding the Games to Antwerp in 1920 and then to Paris in 1924.

He had, then, succeeded in presiding over the establishment of quadrennial international athletic meets that had in many ways conformed to his original ideas and which were, though much smaller, strikingly similar to the periodic international sporting festivals of the middle decades of the twentieth century.

But were they indeed "Olympic Games"? Georges Hébert, another advocate of French athleticism with whom Coubertin cooperated in the 1890s and with whom he later had disputes over the devising of certain curriculum plans in French education, disputed this contention. [25] In 1911 he wrote Coubertin a public letter, saying:

Relative to your so-called Olympic Games, please let me say that it seems to me that you are grandly deluding yourself as to their importance. The present Olympic Games as they are now staged (and you know this as well as I do) have nothing at all in common with the ancient Olympic Games—only the name. Today they actually consist exclusively of a simple exhibition of international athletes. Their influence on all that concerns education in the family, the schools, and in the army really amounts to nothing at all. [26]

We are accustomed to using the term "Olympic Games" in reference to the modern festivals. The ceremony of the modern

"Olympic" pageants (torches, parades, banners, slogans, etc.) purposefully suggest a connection with the rituals at ancient Olympia. The success of these trappings may also suggest that there is no modern system of myth and legend at hand that we can use, aside from the theatrical presentation of sporting contests, which will find wide international acceptance. The festive surroundings of the modern Olympic Games were favored by Coubertin in order to "seduce" important people. The custom of combining spectacle with sport now seduces hundreds of millions of people.

The modern Olympic Games are very much with us and much of their form can be attributed to Coubertin's principles, the belated and extraordinary success of which he could not foretell. Though he favored theatrical surroundings within which an athlete would perform, there was no way for him to anticipate the increasingly elaborate overlays of staging that would become integral parts of the Olympics beginning with the festival in Los Angeles in 1932. In the early years he struggled against proposals to freeze the location of the modern Olympics in Greece, Sweden, or Switzerland. Switching the site every four years meant that the Games could be better controlled from Coubertin's desk, which was also the nerve center of the International Olympic Committee. It should be remembered that until after about 1908 there was no working I.O.C. Only after that date, and then very slowly, did Coubertin begin to consult the princes, millionaires, and elderly bureaucrats (who thought much the same as he did anyway) whose names he had assembled to give the I.O.C. credibility.

Coubertin can also be given credit for the widely inclusive character of the modern Olympic program. We remember that the program at ancient Olympia remained virtually unchanged for centuries. Coubertin rejected any static conceptions for modern sport. Perhaps he never foresaw the bewildering pro- liferation of modern sports and games, but he strongly favored the inclusion of any sport that was internationally practiced by amateurs. From the very beginning he also proposed the inclusion of music and drama festivals in the Olympics. He was throughout his life an ambitious (if unsuccessful) educational reformer and a productive (though unpraised) historian. His most recent biographer has claimed, with some justification, that rather than the fame he has as "Pierre de Coubertin, Reviver of the Olympic Games," he would have preferred (and may deserve) the grander identification, "Pierre de Coubertin, Humanist."[27]

Coubertin's earliest ambitions were to be recognized as a great Frenchman. Yet it was the world as a whole which came to honor him as a great internationalist. This identification of Coubertin as the philosopher of a vague "Olympic idea" was due to enthusiasm for one aspect of his activity as an intellectual and a reformer. And perhaps Coubertin's insistence on periodicity, inclusiveness, festivity, and political independence were more due to his stubbornness than to outstanding vigor or originality of mind.

The Frenchmen he tried to reach ignored rather than rejected him. Subsequently, Frenchmen who have felt, as he did, that their nation was too cerebral and ossified in its traditions have honored him as a prophet and a genius who should have been heeded. It is significant that the public honoring of Coubertin in France—the naming of streets and squares after him, the literature praising him—has grown greatly since 1945 when France had to examine herself after a debacle comparable to the one in 1870 that inspired young Pierre de Coubertin to attempt to revive French energies.

Coubertin was always an aristocrat in temperament. He was rarely tolerant of others. In Paris when he was young, his eagerness to pursue the victims of accusations of professionalism kept him perpetually in disputes with the officials of minor sporting bodies. He was always fighting with someone. He saw enemies "where there were none. . . . a sort of persecution complex. He believed so strongly in Olympism that he was willing to make concessions in writing and in action to anyone . . . as long as the Games continued."[28]

As he aged, the continual worsening of his personal circumstances increased his isolation and bitterness. During World War I he volunteered for military service, but instead was sent off to inspect the physical education programs of French provincial lycées. He never acquired the bourgeois respect for money. His fortune, already weakened by the outlays for propaganda and festivities to promote Anglo-Saxon sport, was gravely eroded by the inflation. He released his footman and other servants and sold the family hotel on the rue Oudinot in 1918. His favorite sister-in-law was killed in the German bombardment of Paris. His two nephews were lost in combat. The loss of these youths was especially sad for him, since it meant the end of the line of the Frédy-Coubertins. Pierre had had a son at the end of the year 1896. The boy was lively and healthy until a severe case of sunstroke at the age of two sent him into a catatonic state from which he never recovered. This calamity, in turn, snapped the equilibrium of the mother, who became a compulsive shrew. Since his daughter, who gave Pierre some joy, was also unstable and sometimes required psychiatric care, the mother guarded her small fortune to maintain the family. Pierre de Coubertin squandered everything. During the last years of his life he was destitute. His wife (she died in 1963 aged 101) refused to give him pocket money.[29]

When the family moved to Switzerland in 1918, they took the archives of the Olympic movement with them. Coubertin wrote his last works in a small office (still preserved as he knew it) in a mansion given to the International Olympic Committee by the city of Lausanne. He accused associates of stealing his ideas. His poverty and paranoia (he tended to write angry public letters) isolated him ever more from his co-workers and then from international assemblies. In the 1920s the I.O.C. evolved from being his usable fiction into a working body of conservative gentlemen of the world who were (and have remained) dedicated to preserving the founder's reputation, at least as it bears on the Olympic Games.

He was a relic and a mythical figure long before his death. His views had no influence upon the awarding of the eleventh modern Olympics to Berlin for the Games of 1936, but he expressed satisfaction at the reports of the lavish pagan festival planned by the National Socialists. The new Germans honored him gratefully as a titan of ideas. During the opening ceremony on August 1, 1936, the Nazis demanded hushed reverence as they played a recording of his voice to an assembly of 110,000 people in their new stadium. But they kept the sour old man in Switzerland.

A long-planned, final piece of theater went into effect after he died. On September 25, 1937, he was walking at his usual rapid pace in the Parc de Lagrange in Geneva. Suddenly he swept his hand to his chest, and then, efficiently and alone, he was dead. In keeping with a provision in his will, his body was buried in Lausanne and the heart that had at last failed him was cut from his body to be placed in an urn and buried in the sacred soil of ancient Olympia in Greece.

NOTES

1: THE OLYMPIC GAMES IN ANTIQUITY

1. The debate over the origins of the Olympic Games is one that has preoccupied sports historians. A school of German historians—see especially Karl Meuli, "Der Ursprung der Olympischen Spiele," *Die Antike*, XVII (1941), 197 ff., and the discussion in Ulrich Popplow, *Leibesübungen und Leibeserziehung in der griechischen Antike* (4th ed.; Schorndorf bei Stuttgart: Karl Hofmann, 1967), pp. 31–52—claims that all the ancient athletic festivals are descended from combats and sacrifices held on the occasions of the funerals of heroes. Much more pragmatic is the claim of E. Norman Gardiner in *Athletics of the Ancient World* (Oxford: Clarendon, 1930) that for aristocratic Greek males the cultic observations were also social occasions which provided opportunities for contests of physical skill which they loved. The contests, of which we have many examples in the *Odyssey* and the *Iliad*, gradually became regularized at Olympia, Delphi, Sparta, and many other places. Why the Greeks adopted and formalized their peculiar sports is also a subject for much speculation, which must be passed over here.

2. Essential for all monographs on Olympia and the Games are the detailed reports of the Prussian (later German) archaeological expeditions of 1875–1881 (published in 1890–1897), 1936–1942, and 1952–1966. Citations for the various reports can be found in the works by Drees, Herrmann, and Gardiner cited below. A handy summary of the archaeological work at Olympia is the catalog, *100 Jahre deutsche Ausgrabungen in Olympia* (München: Prestel, 1972), published for an exhibition held in Munich in the summer and fall of 1972. This catalog has a useful bibliography on the ancient Olympics (pp. 134–135).

3. In the following discussion I am heavily indebted to several excellent books on the ancient Olympic Games: Ludwig Drees, *Olympia: Gotter, Kunstler und Athleten* (Stuttgart: W. Kohlhammer, 1967; English translation, New York: Praeger, 1968); Hans-Volkmar Herrmann, *Olympia: Heiligtum und Wettkampfstätte* (München: Hirmer, 1972); Edward Norman Gardiner, *Olympia: Its History and Remains* (Oxford: Clarendon, 1925). These three

books, as well as most others, are heavily dependent upon the German archaeological reports mentioned in note 2 above. The best literary source for the festival at Olympia is Pausanias's *Description of Greece*, Books V and VI, available in the Loeb Classical Library. An author who distrusts archaeologically based speculation, and who favors speculation based on literary sources for ancient athletics, is H. A. Harris. See his *Greek Athletes and Athletics* (London: Hutchinson, 1964) and his *Sport in Greece and Rome* (London: Thames and Hudson, 1972).

4. I shall follow the practice of previous writers on Olympia and lean very heavily on Pausanias, who was more interested in geographical description than chronology and who wrote his description of Olympia about 200 B.C. The order of events and their rules did vary over the centuries of Olympia's grandeur, and it seems certain that near the beginning of Olympia's long history, and at the end, the program was shorter. For most of Olympia's history these were also contests for trumpeters and heralds.

5. Pausanias, V, 24, 9. From Loeb Classical Library, trans. W. H. S. Jones and H. A. Ormerod.

6. Since this book is essentially about modern sport, it would be idle to review here the controversies among the sports historians over the scoring system in the ancient pentathlon. From slim evidence, different archaeologists and philologists have deduced widely differing, intricate methods which they defend with pride and scorn for that of others. See, for example, the discussion in Harris, *Greek Athletes and Athletics*, and in Gerhard Lukas, *Die Körperkultur in frühen Epochen der Menschheitsentwicklung* (Berlin: Sportverlag, 1969) pp. 88–92.

7. As they are for many aspects of Greek sport. I have tried to present only those aspects of ancient sport and the sports festivals which seem to be matters of general agreement among the specialists whose work I am plundering.

8. For example, in the *Iliad* Athena answers the prayers of her favorite, Odysseus, and trips the swifter Aias during the footrace at the funeral games for Patroclus.

9. I am not aware of any modern empirical research that would test these techniques, which conceivably could have more than a placebo effect.

10. The Spartans had some footraces for girls. The literary sources for the claims that there were also festivals for women are scanty and equivocal. See the discussion in Harris, *Greek Athletes and Athletics*, pp. 179–186.

11. In a large city, various athletic facilities had reputations that drew to them a clientele that would prefer one or more of the activities listed.

12. The monumental two-volume work published in 1841 by Johann Heinrich Kraus, *Die Gymnastik und Agonistik der Hellenen* (Leipzig: Johann A. Barth, 1841; repr., Hildesheim: Georg Olms, 1972), was based on sources available at that time and has been used directly or indirectly by all sports historians since then.

13. The sole visual representation of what may be a ball game shows two youths with hockey sticks on a sixth-century statue base presently in the

National Museum in Athens. I myself am unconvinced that what is depicted is a team game.

14. See Erwin Mehl, *Antike Swimkunst* (München: Heimeran, 1927).

15. A good if rather gullible survey occurs on pp. 89–137 of Ulrich Popplow, cited in n. 1 above.

16. See, for example, Euripides' denunciation of athletes in his fragment, *Autolycus*.

17. See the discussion in Gardiner, *Athletics of the Ancient World*, p. 121.

18. See Joze Kastelik, *Situalakunst: Meisterschöpfungen prähistorischer Bronzearbeit* (Wien: Schrollenverlag, 1964), p. xxxiv.

19. Quoted in Harris, *Sport in Greece and Rome*, p. 53.

20. All these activities were aspects of Augustus's totalitarian intention to assure that the prestige accruing to the hosts of political or quasi-political festivals would accrue to the emperor alone.

21. The several surviving Greek stadiums were all built rather late and never equaled in splendor the elaborate Roman arenas. Though we can still see many Roman hippodromes, no Greek hippodromes survive because they were merely open fields with starting gates and a rounding column.

22. In the following discussion, I am indebted to Michael Grant, *Gladiators* (New York: Delacorte, 1967).

23. The brigand and former slave and gladiator Spartacus led his rebellion from Capua in 73 B.C.

24. I am running ahead of the story here. Most modern so-called sport scholarship is polemical. The authors are usually committed physical educationalists who are alarmed at the slowness with which their mission proceeds. The exaggerated praise of antique sport is a veiled criticism, if not of the Christian era, of the insufficient enthusiasm for sport that has come with it. For more on this, see Alois Koch, *Die Leibesübungen im Urteil der antiken und frühchristlichen Anthropologie* (Schorndorf bei Stuttgart: Karl Hofmann, 1965).

25. A modern scholar has concluded from the frequency and aptness of his sporting metaphors that Saint Paul was not antiathletic, or at least was an athlete himself in his youth. See Harris, *Greek Athletics and Athletes*, pp. 129–135.

26. One is reminded of the demand in our days for seats to observe the Passion play at Oberammergau.

27. Glanville Downey, *Ancient Antioch* (Princeton: Princeton University Press, 1963), p. 44.

2: PROPOSALS FOR REVIVAL

1. See the discussion in H. A. Harris, *Great Athletes and Athletics* (London: Hutchinson, 1964) pp. 54–55.

2. Charles Homer Haskins, *The Latin Literature of Sport*, Vol. V in *Studies in Medieval Culture* (New York: Frederick Ungar, 1958), p. 107.

3. "Sportsmen wrote in Latin and hunted and fought in the vernacular" (ibid., p. 108).

4. Henning Eichberg, *Der Weg des Sports in die industrielle Zivilisation* (Baden-Baden: Nomos, 1973), p. 61.

5. Louis Sebastian Mercier quoted in J. J. Jusserand, *Les sports et jeux d'exercise dans l'ancienne France* (Paris: Plon, 1901), p. 415.

6. Ibid, p. 417.

7. From a letter of March 19, 1778, quoted in ibid, p. 418.

8. Charles Du Fresne Du Cange, *Glossarium Mediae et Infimae Latinitatis . . .*, of which there have been various editions since 1678. See the 1954 Graz edition, Vol. 6, p. 43.

9. Pergolesi's overture "L'Olympique" and Mouret's ballet music, "Les jeux olympiques."

10. Quoted at length in Jusserand, *Les sports et jeux*, p. 419.

11. Paul Robert, *Dictionnaire alphabetique et analogique de la langue française* (Paris: Presses Universitaires de la France), IV, 892.

12. Emile Littré, *Dictionnaire de la langue française* (Paris: Pauvert, 1962——), V, 1003.

13. See the discussions in the *Oxford English Dictionary* (rev. ed., Oxford: Oxford University, 1933), vol. 8, p. 107. My claims for the popularity of the word in French and English leave out the rather special literature of German philology and archaeology.

14. Lodewyk Bendikson, "Forgotten Olympics in King James' Reign," *Game and Gossip*, X, no. 5 (1932), 7.

15. Matthew Walbancke, ed., *Annalia Dubrensia: Upon the yeerely celebration of Mr. Robert Dover's Olympicke games upon Cotswold-Hills* (London: R. Raworth, 1636).

16. Ibid.

17. See Alfred E. Robbins, "Olympic Games in England," *Notes and Queries*, ser. 10, X (Aug. 22, 1908), 147.

18. See his "Les jeux olympiques à Much Wenlock," *La revue athlétique*, I, no. 12 (Dec. 25, 1890), 705–712. This quotation is from the English version of the article which appeared in the *Review of Reviews* (New York) in January, 1897, p. 63.

19. "The Pan-Britannic Gathering," *Nineteenth Century*, XXIV (July, 1893), 86.

20. Cited in J. Astley Cooper, "An Anglo-Saxon Olympiad, *Nineteenth Century*, XXXII (Sept., 1892), 381. For a postmortem on these unrealized projects, see Cooper's "The Olympic Games: What Has Been Done and What Remains to be Done," *Nineteenth Century*, LXIII (June, 1908), 1011–1021. In 1908 the author was more gruffly racist. He called the Athens Games of 1896 "a hybrid, babel gathering."

21. Cooper, "An Anglo-Saxon Olympiad," p. 386.

22. "Henry Laurens on the Olympic Games," *South Carolina Historical Magazine*, LXI (July, 1960), 146–147.

23. Jean Ketseas, "A Restatement," *Bulletin du comité international olympique*, no. 83 (Aug., 1963), p. 56.

24. Georges M. Bourdon, "Athènes essaye de faire revivre Olympie," *Les jeux de 8ᵉ Olympiade* (Paris: Comité olympique français, 1924), p. 20.

25. I. E. Chrysafe, *Oi synchronoi diethneis olympiakoi Agones* (Athenai: Biblioteke tes Epitropes ton olympiakon Agonon, 1930).

26. Sir John Pentland Mahaffey, "The Olympic Games in Athens in 1875," *Macmillan's Magazine*, XXXII (1875), 325.

27. Ibid., pp. 326–327.

28. See Berthold Fellmann, "Die Wiederentdeckung Olympias," *100 Jahre deutsche Ausgrabungen in Olympia* (München: Prestel, 1972), pp. 27–34. See also Joachim Gerstenberg, *Die Wiedergewinnung Olympias als Stätte und Idee* (Baden-Baden: Kairos, 1949).

29. See Abel Blouet, *Expédition scientifique de Morée*, I (Paris: Didot, 1831), 56 ff., pl. 56–78.

30. Johann Heinrich Krause, *Theagenes: Oder, Wissenschaftliche Darstellung der Gymnastik, Agonistik und Festspiele der Hellenen* (Halle: Verfasser, 1835); *Olympia: Oder Darstellung der grossen olympischen Spiele . . .* (Wien: Beck, 1938); *Die Gymnastik und Agonistik der Hellenen aus den Schrift- und Bildwerken des Altertums . . .* (2 vols., Leipzig: Barth, 1841). Krause's collection of the available literary and other materials has been used, directly or indirectly, by almost all subsequent historians of classical sport.

31. Quoted in *100 Jahre deutsche Ausgrabungen in Olympia*, p. 32.

32. Ibid.

33. The contract (quoted at length in ibid., pp. 33-34) was a model for all later contracts between the Greeks and foreign archaeologists.

34. Or Bonn. Under the leadership of Carl Diem the Germans began new excavations in 1937. These were interrupted in 1942 and recommenced by the Federal Republic in 1952. The eight volumes (so far) of reports for the twentieth-century excavations bear the title, *Berichte über die Ausgrabungen in Olympia* (1937——).

35. Edward Norman Gardiner's first book, *Greek Athletic Sports and Festivals* (London: Macmillan, 1910), was written primarily to acquaint an English-speaking audience with the results of German scholarship.

36. See Eliza Marian Butler, *The Tyranny of Greece over Germany* (Cambridge: Cambridge University Press, 1935), and Fritz Ernst, *Der Klassizismus in Italien, Frankreich und Deutschland* (Zürich: Amalthea, 1924).

37. "Turning" (*Turnen*) is a uniquely German complex of intellectual and educational (as well as athletic) developments. I will not translate "turning" as "gymnastics," as is usually done in American and British writing. The Germans themselves use *Gymnastik* to describe developments that were comtemporaneous and comparable, but were separate and Scandinavian.

38. The German literature on the subject is detailed and vast. See the long critical essay by Hajo Bernett, *Die pädagogische Neugestaltung der bürgerlichen Leibesübungen durch die Philanthropen* (Schorndorf bei Stuttgart: Karl Hofmann, 1960). See also the discussion in Eichberg, op. cit., pp. 37–38.

39. See Walter Umminger, *Die Olympischen Spiele der Neuzeit* (Dortmund: Olympischen Sportverlag, 1969), p. 10.

40. Without the notice of intellectuals or academics, either. This explains the astonishing difference in quality and quantity between German and Anglo-Saxon sports scholarship.

41. See Richard D. Mandell, *Paris 1900: The Great World's Fair* (Toronto: University of Toronto Press, 1967).

42. By the 1890s there was also the analogous and powerful Sokol movement among the Czechs. Plans were afoot for a similar movement (later realized) among Zionists.

43. For speculation as to the distant origins of modern English sport, see Dennis Brailsford, *Sport and Society: Elizabeth to Anne* (London: Routledge and Kegan Paul, 1969). See also Maria Kloeren, *Kultursoziologische Untersuchungen zum England des sechzehnten bis achtzehnten Jahrhunderts* (Leipzig: Tauchnitz, 1935). For information on the codification and spread of English sport, see Albert Hirn, *Ursprung und Wesen des Sports* (Berlin: Weidmann, 1936).

44. And profitable—as with league baseball and, later, professional boxing, running, and cycling.

45. *Nation*, LVII (Dec., 1893), 423.

3: COUBERTIN

1. Carl Diem, "Pierre de Coubertin's Ancestry," *Bulletin du Comité international olympique* (Jan. 15, 1952).

2. Most of these early biographical details are taken from Marie-Thérèse Eyquem, *Pierre de Coubertin: L'Épopée olympique* (Paris: Calmann-Lévy, 1966), pp. 9–17.

3. Ibid.

4. See the discussions in Claude Digeon, *La crise allemande de la pensée française (1870–1914)* (Paris: Presses universitaires de la France, 1959), esp. "La menace allemande," pp. 451–488.

5. Pierre de Coubertin, *Batailles de l'éducation: Une campagne de vingt-et-un ans, 1887–1908* (Paris: Librairie de l'éducation physique, 1908), pp. 1–2.

6. Hippolyte Taine, *Notes on England*, trans. with introduction by Edward Hyams (London: Thames and Hudson, 1957), pp. 102–104.

7. A hagiographer of the modern Olympic movement has established that Coubertin was himself a philosopher of considerable stature and insinuates that he was inspired by all the European greats from Hegel and Michelet to Bergson and Nietzsche. See Rudolf Malter, *Der Olympismus Pierre de Coubertin's: Eine kritische Studie zu Idee der modernen Olympischen Spiele und des Sports* (Köln: Carl-Diem-Institut, 1969). A bitter critic of the modern Olympic movement and a young follower of the "Frankfurt sociologists" claims that the most influential philosophical influence on Coubertin was August Comte. See Ulrike Prokop, *Sociologie der Olympischen Spiele*

(Munich: Carl Hanser, 1971). Neither of these efforts seems to be based upon a reading of Coubertin's early work. Coubertin himself claimed that he was most inspired by Thomas Arnold, but it is also clear that he had read little of Arnold's writing.

Eyquem's biography, which is based on some primary sources and a chronological ordering of Coubertin's writing, is the best yet. But almost everything written on Coubertin is done by physical educationalists who wish to fashion their own Coubertin to promote their own plans to reform education or sport.

8. T. W. Bamford, *Thomas Arnold* (London: Cresset, 1960), p. 189. See chap. vi, "The Growth of the Arnold Legend," pp. 175–190, for more on this subject.

9. Bamford, *op. cit.*, is a good, critical biography.

10. London: Chatto and Windus, 1918.

11. Eyquem, *Pierre de Coubertin*, p. 32.

12. Ibid., pp. 44–45.

13. Coubertin's record of the trip was published as *Universités transatlantiques* (Paris: Hachette, 1890).

14. Quoted in John Apostal Lucas, "Baron Pierre de Coubertin and the Formative Years of the Modern International Olympic Movement, 1883–1896" (Ph.D. dissertation, University of Maryland, 1962), pp. 68–69.

15. *Les Batailles de l'éducation physique*, p. 55.

16. See *Le roman d'un rallié*, published under the pseudonym "Georges Hohrod" (Auxerre: Albert Lanier, 1902).

17. "Contradictions of Modern France," *Fortnightly Review*, LXIII March, 1898), 352.

18. There are two bibliographies of Coubertin's writings: *Répertoire des écrits, discours et conférences de Coubertin* ("Publié a l'occasion de sa 70me année en hommage des comités olympiques d'Egypte, de Grèce, de Lettonie, de Portugal, de Suède et Suisse et du Bureau International de Pedagogie Sportive"); "Bibliographie der Werke Baron Pierre de Coubertin's . . .," in Pierre de Coubertin, *Der Olympische Gedanke* (Cologne: Carl-Diem-Institut, 1967), pp. 157–164 (also published in a French and an English edition). The latter bibliography does not include Coubertin's *Histoire universelle*.

19. Eyquem (*Pierre de Coubertin*, p. 103) has also remarked on this.

20. *The Evolution of France under the Third Republic* (New York: Thomas Y. Crowell, 1897).

21. This information can be gleaned from the Albert Shaw letterbook in the Manuscript Division of the New York Public Library. Coubertin wrote for the American *Review of Reviews* while Shaw was editor.

22. Significantly, Coubertin's memoirs published in 1909 were called *Les batailles de l'éducation physique*.

23. See Eugen Weber, "Gymnastics and Sport in *fin de siècle* France: Opium of the Classes?" *American Historical Review* (Feb., 1971), 70–98; and

"Pierre de Coubertin and the Introduction of Organized Sport in France," *Journal of Contemporary History*, V, no. 2 (1970), 3–26.

24. See the accusations made against Coubertin by Willibald Gebhardt, first German member of the "International Olympic Committee" after the Olympics of 1900, in *Dokumente zur Frühgeschichte der Olympischen Spiele* (Cologne: Carl-Diem-Institut, 1970), pp. 132–133 and notes.

25. "La question des parfums," *Revue olympique*, no. 56 (Aug., 1910), pp. 123–125.

26. *Revue olympique*, no. 87, pp. 45–46.

27. Alex Natan, "Sport and Politics," *in* Alex Natan, ed., *Sport and Society* (London: Bowes and Bowes, 1958), p. 53

28. Both Malter (*Der Olympismus Pierre de Coubertin's*, pp. 16–18) and Prokop (*Soziologie der Olympischen Spiele*, pp. 44–50) have also remarked on this.

29. I have not found solid proof for this statement, and I believe that Coubertin was much impressed with the theatrical presentations of American football and baseball games when he traveled in the United States in 1889.

30. "The Olympic Games of 1896," *Century*, LXIII, no. 1 (Nov., 1896), 50–53.

4: ORGANIZATION

1. Marie-Thérèse Eyquem, *Pierre de Coubertin: L'Épopée Olympique* (Paris: Calmann-Lévy, 1966), p. 66.

2. Pierre de Coubertin, *Les batailles de l'éducation physique: Une campagne de vingt-et-un ans 1887–1908* (Paris: Librairie de l'éducation physique, 1908), p. 31.

3. Ibid., p. 40.

4. Ibid., p. 39.

5. Ibid., p. 45.

6. Paschal Grousset quoted in ibid., p. 42.

7. Ibid., p. 50.

8. See chap. 2.

9. Eugen Weber, "Pierre de Coubertin and the Introduction of Organized Sport in France," *Journal of Contemporary History*, V, no. 2 (1970), 3–26; and "Gymnastics and Sports in *fin de siècle* France: Opium of the Classes?" *American Historical Review*, LXXVI, no. 1 (Feb., 1971), 70–98.

10. Coubertin, *Les batailles*, p. 55.

11. Quoted in Eyquem, *Pierre de Coubertin*, p. 128.

12. Coubertin, *Les batailles*, p. 67.

13. Jusserand later published *Les sports et jeux d'exercise dans l'ancienne France* (Paris: Plon, 1901).

14. Eyquem, *Pierre de Coubertin*, p. 129.

15. Quoted in ibid., p. 131. The Olympic historians (including Eyquem) claim that Coubertin's was the first public proposal by anyone for a revival of the Olympic Games.

16. Coubertin, *Les batailles*, p. 83.

17. *Dictionary of American Biography* (New York: Scribners, 1935–1936), IX, 214.

18. *The Life of Napoleon Bonaparte* (4 vols.; New York: Century, 1896).

19. Eyquem, *Pierre de Coubertin*, p. 133.

20. Reprinted in Pierre de Coubertin, *L'Idée olympique* (Cologne: Carl-Diem-Institut, 1967), pp. 3–5.

21. Schwarzkoppen was contemporaneously in the course of passing stolen secret documents over to Berlin. Some French generals hastily (and incorrectly) deduced that Schwarzkoppen's contact was Alfred Dreyfus, thus beginning the Dreyfus affair.

22. Eyquem, *Pierre de Coubertin*, p. 135.

23. See Theodore Reinach, "Une page de musique grecque," *La Revue de Paris*, I, no. 10 (June 15, 1894), 204–224.

24. Coubertin's claim in the final issue of his *Bulletin du Comité international des jeux olympique* (July, 1894), p. 2. The meeting was noticed in a few newspapers (see the *New York Times* of June 17, 1894, or *The Times* [London] of June 19, 1894) but Coubertin is the source for the emotional atmosphere.

25. *Revue de Paris*, I, no. 10, pp. 170–184. This same issue contained the article on the "Ode to Apollo."

26. Speech given in full in Coubertin, *L'Idée olympique*, pp. 5–7.

27. Some versions of this story have Bikelas as the initiator of the suggestion of Athens in 1896. Coubertin later published (*Les batailles*, p. 98) a note to him from Bikelas in which Bikelas wrote, "I did not see you after the session so I could not say how much I was touched by your suggestion to begin with Athens. I regret not having the opportunity to support you more warmly." It seems to me likely that there must have been some preliminary discussions before the motion at the last banquet. Coubertin could assimilate a vaguely envisaged "marathon," but was unlikely to decide impulsively on the site and date of the first modern Olympic Games. The fact that the Greek king accepted the invitation at once suggests that Bikelas, like Balck, had a mandate when he left for Paris and that Coubertin was aware of it and was prepared to act on it.

28. Paul Shorey, "Can we Revive the Olympic Games?" *Forum*, XIX (May, 1895), 317–323.

29. "The Latest Athletic Whim," *Spectator*, LXXII, no. 3443 (June 23, 1894), 851–852.

30. See the articles and republished correspondence in *Dokumente zur Frühgeschichte der Olympischen Spiele* (Cologne: Carl-Diem-Institut, 1970), pp. 1–19.

31. Gebhardt has since been made a hero in German sports historiography. See Erke Hamer, *Willibald Gebhardt, 1861–1921* (Cologne: Carl-Diem-Institut, 1971).

32. Taken from Gebhardt's translation in his *Soll Deutschland sich an den olympischen Spielen teilnehmen* (Berlin: K. Siegismund, 1896), pp. 122–124, and reprinted in *Dokumente zur Frühgeschichte*, p. 19.

33. *Zentral-Ausschluss zur Forderung der Jugend und Volkspiele.*

5: ATHENS GETS READY

1. Letter from Coubertin in Bikelas correspondence in the Coubertin archives at the headquarters of the International Olympic Committee in Lausanne.

2. Full text given in Pierre de Coubertin, *Les batailles de l'éducation physique: Une campagne de vingt-et-un ans* (Paris: Librairie de l'éducation physique, 1908), pp. 109–111.

3. Marie-Thérèse Eyquem, *Pierre de Coubertin: L'Épopée olympique* (Paris: Calmann-Lévy, 1966), p. 142.

4. Pierre de Coubertin, *Souvenirs d'Amérique et de Grèce* (Paris: Hachette, 1896), p. 119.

5. Coubertin, *Les batailles*, p. 112.

6. Ibid., p. 115.

7. Speech given in *Bulletin du Comité international des Jeux olympiques*, II, no. 3 (January, 1895), 4.

8. Ibid.

9. Coubertin, *Mémoires olympiques* (Lausanne: B.I.P.S., 1931), p. 26.

10. The key dispute was over military discipline. Coubertin (*Les batailles*, p. 117) suggested that Olympism was the issue.

11. Coubertin, *Les batailles*, p. 120.

12. Ibid., p. 123.

13. *Les jeux olympiques: 776 av. J.C.–1896* (Athens: Beck, 1896), II, 19–23. This is the official report of the Games of 1896. Text is in Greek, French, and English.

14. Coubertin, *Souvenirs*, p. 147.

15. Coubertin, *Mémoires olympiques*, pp. 34–35.

16. *Jahrbuch für Volks- und Jugendspiele* quoted in *Dokumente zur Frühgeschichte der olympischen Spiele* (Cologne: Carl-Diem-Institut, 1970), p. 71.

17. Given in Gebhardt's letter to Coubertin of January 20, 1896, printed in *Dokumente*, p. 57.

18. See letter, ibid.

19. "Comité hellène a jamais cru paroles attribuées à vous initiateur renaissance jeux olympiques," (Coubertin, *Les batailles*, p. 125).

20. Ibid., pp. 126–127. This is, however, contradicted in Coubertin's correspondence. He was bitter and remained so for many years.

21. G. S. Robertson, "The Olympic Games by a Competitor and Prize Winner," *Fortnightly Review*, CCCLIV (June 1, 1896), 950.

22. Ibid., p. 944.

23. P. Bigelow in *New York Times*, March 29, 1896, pp. 32–36.

24. Graham and Ellery H. Clark were later coauthors of *Practical Track and Field Athletics* (New York: Duffield, 1910).

25. Ellery H. Clark, *Reminiscences of an Athlete: Twenty Years on Track and Field* (Boston: Houghton Mifflin, 1911), p. 124.

26. Charles B. Saunders, "Olympic Princetonians," *Princeton Alumni*, LVII, no. 12 (Dec. 7, 1956), 5. Connolly was readmitted and was awarded a major "H" at the fiftieth reunion of his class in 1949.

27. From an undatable newspaper clipping in the scrapbooks of Francis A. Lane. The scrapbooks are in the archives at Princeton University.

28. Ibid.

29. Clark, *Reminiscences*, p. 127.

30. Ibid., p. 129.

31. Robertson, "The Olympic Games," p. 953.

32. Robertson commented (ibid., p. 954): "The committee were fortunate in not having to deal with a northcountry football crowd."

6: THE ATHENS GAMES

1. From the English version of the official report. The original Greek and a French translation are given in *Les jeux olympiques: 776 av. J.C.–1896* (Athens: Beck, 1896), II, 56 (henceforth cited as *Jeux olympiques*).

2. George Horton, "The Recent Olympic Games," *Bostonian*, IV, no. 4 (July, 1896), 220. For another version of this incident, see Ellery H. Clark, *Reminiscences of an Athlete: Twenty Years on Track and Field* (New York: Houghton Mifflin, 1911), p. 130.

3. The winning discus can still be seen in the trophy case at the main Princeton gymnasium.

4. Thomas P. Curtis, "The Glory That Was Greece," *Sportsman*, XII, no. 1 (July, 1932), 22.

5. Curiously and erroneously, Gouskos has been subsequently identified as Garrett's competitor in the discus contest of the preceding day. This mistake is no doubt owing to the partly fictional story of the 1896 Games by James Connolly, the successful competitor in Athens who later became a noted writer of, among other things, stories of the sea. What Connolly did was fictionally to fuse the discus and shot–putting events. See his novel, *Olympic Victor: A Story of the Modern Games* (New York, 1908), which was condensed and serialized in *Scribner's Magazine* in July, August, and September of 1908. Connolly also portrayed Gouskos as a close friend of the winner of the marathon.

6. *Jeux olympiques*, II, 66.

7. Possibly apocryphal, but documentable in Curtis, "The Glory That Was Greece," p. 22. The gentleman from Boston had probably told the anecdotes in this autobiographical article many times before they were published thirty-six years after the events. We can be sure they became funnier with each repetition.

8. *Jeux olympiques*, II, 76.

9. Curtis, "The Glory That Was Greece," p. 22. The sole English report we

have on the 1896 Games insists that Goulding was the better man. See G. S. Robertson, "The Olympic Games by a Competitor and a Prize Winner," *Fortnightly Review*, CCCLIV (June 1, 1896), 947. Robertson also classified Flack, the Australian runner, as English.

10. The accepted version of the original marathon is attributable to Robert Browning's poem "Pheidippides" in his *Dramatic Idylls*. Browning freely used the name of the runner dispatched by the Athenians before the battle of Marathon to request aid from Sparta. This hero, Pheidippides, was fictionally merged with the purported bearer of the glad news of victory, whose name has always been unknown and who may have never run, much less perished so dramatically, in the first place.

11. Connolly cast, as Loues's rival, the erstwhile nasty village bully who shouts back at the gaining Loues, "Rather a Turk than you!" (see "Olympic Victor," *Scribner's Magazine* [1908], pp. 360–362).

12. Coubertin wrote that the lady seated next to him sent down her gold watch and pearls ("The Olympic Games of 1896," *Century Magazine*, LIII, no. 1 [Nov., 1896], 46).

13. Curtis, "The Glory That Was Greece," p. 22.

14. Almost all these romantic possibilities were combined in Connolly's *Olympic Victor*.

15. Robertson, "The Olympic Games," p. 946.

16. Curtis, "The Glory That Was Greece," p. 56.

17. Curtis (ibid.) suggested that if some Yalies had been there, they might have responded with their cheer from Aristophanes' "Frog Chorus"—but that the Greeks would not have understood, Greeks though they were.

18. Quoted by Rufus B. Richardson, "The New Olympian Games," *Scribner's Magazine*, XX, no. 3 (Sept., 1896), 276.

19. Ibid., p. 281.

20. Ibid., p. 277.

21. The program is in the scrapbooks of Francis A. Lane. The scrapbooks are in the archives at Princeton University.

22. Curtis, "The Glory That Was Greece," p. 56. Again possibly apocryphal, but I have found no other record of Gardiner Williams's performance.

23. Richardson, "The New Olympic Games," p. 269.

24. The menu is in the Lane scrapbooks at Princeton.

25. *Jeux olympiques*, II, 100.

26. Ibid., p. 101.

27. Curtis, "The Glory That Was Greece," p. 56.

7: AFTER THE GAMES

1. *Les jeux olympiques: 776 av. J.C.–1896* (Athens: Beck, 1896), II, 100.

2. *Les batailles de l'éducation physique: Une campagne de vingt-et-un ans 1887–1908* (Paris: Librairie de l'éducation physique, 1908), p. 127.

3. Estimates varied widely as to the numbers of foreigners. Some Greek newspapers claimed they numbered twenty thousand. G. S. Robertson, the

English poet who read a Pindaric ode before King George, estimated one thousand in "The Olympic Games by a Competitor and a Prize Winner," *Fortnightly Review*, CCCLIV (June 1, 1896), 955.

4. See the discussion in William L. Langer, *The Diplomacy of Imperialism 1890–1902*, I (New York: Knopf, 1935), 356–378.

5. For a kinder appraisal of Constantine I see Edouard Driault, *Le roi Constantin* (Versailles: privately printed, 1930).

6. For a discussion of this problem see Henning Eichberg, "Der Beginn des modernen Leistens," *Sportwissenschaft*, IV, no. 1 (1974), 21–48.

7. Letter dated September 6, 1896, published in an unplaceable and undatable *Evening Sun*. The clipping is in Francis Lane's scrapbook in the archives at Princeton University.

8. Clippings from Francis Lane's scrapbooks.

9. Undatable clipping from *Daily Princetonian* in Francis Lane's scrapbooks.

10. *Boston Daily Globe*, May 7, 1896.

11. Ibid., May 8, 1896.

12. See William Hemmingway, "How Canada Started the Marathon Craze," *Harper's Weekly*, LIII (May 1, 1909), 24. Hemmingway's claims were pretty well demolished by James E. Sullivan, "The Marathon Craze," ibid., LIII (May 15, 1909), 6.

13. Robertson, "The Olympic Games," pp. 944–957.

14. Citations for these colorless summaries may be found in the bibliographical notes (*Anmerkungen*) in *Dokumente zur Frühgeschichte der Olympischen Spiele* (Cologne: Carl-Diem-Institut, 1940), pp. 197–219. Later interviews with the German, Austrian, and Hungarian athletes, by then old men, contain grotesque exaggerations. See, for example, the series of articles by Alfred Hajos, "Erinnerungen eines Olympiasieger's," *Olympisches Feuer*, VI (1956).

15. "The Olympic Games of 1896," *Century*, LXIII, no. 1 (Nov., 1896), 39–53.

16. Coubertin, *Mémoires olympiques* (Lausanne: Bureau international de pedagogie sportive, 1931), pp. 48–49.

17. See M. de Chasseloup-Laubat, "Congrès international de l'éducation physique," in *Rapport général sur les congrès de l'Exposition* (Paris: Imprimerie nationale, 1906), pp. 660–667.

18. Coubertin, *Mémoires olympiques*, p. 47.

19. Analogously, the Republic itself, in a turmoil about the Dreyfus affair, had Captain Dreyfus retried in provincial Rennes in August and September, 1898, in order to escape the overheated political atmosphere of Paris. See Coubertin's explanation for the change of site in his *Les batailles*, pp. 133.

20. *Mémoires olympiques*, p. 50.

21. Ibid., pp. 51–53.

22. Ibid., p. 54.

23. See the accusations of Willibald Gebhardt in *Dokumente zur Frühgeschichte*.

24. Coubertin, *Mémoires olympiques*, p. 59.

25. See the discussion in **Marie-Thérèse** Eyquem, *Pierre de Coubertin: L'Épopée olympique* (Paris: Calmann-Lévy, 1966), pp. 116–117.

26. Letter in *Bulletin du Comité international olympique*, no. 80 (Nov. 15, 1962), pp. 25–26.

27. Eyquem, *Pierre de Coubertin*, p. 125.

28. Mme Zanchi, former associate of Coubertin and former secretary of the International Committee, as quoted in John A. Lucas, "Baron Pierre de Coubertin and the Formative Years of the Modern International Olympic Movement" (Ph.D. dissertation, University of Maryland, 1962), p. 68.

29. Author's interview with Mme Zanchi in the summer of 1969.

INDEX